Scotland

Scotland

BY R. CONRAD STEIN

Enchantment of the World
Second Series

Children's Press®

A Division of Scholastic Inc.

NEW YORK   TORONTO   LONDON   AUCKLAND   SYDNEY
MEXICO CITY   NEW DELHI   HONG KONG
DANBURY, CONNECTICUT

Frontispiece: A castle in the Scottish highlands

Consultant: Ruth Mitchell-Pitts, Ph.D., Associate Director, Center for European Studies, University of North Carolina at Chapel Hill

Please note: *All statistics are as up-to-date as possible at the time of publication.*

Book Production by Herman Adler Design

Library of Congress Cataloging-in-Publication Data

Stein, R. Conrad
    Scotland / by R. Conrad Stein
      p. cm. — (Enchantment of the world. Second series)
    Includes bibliographical references and index.
    ISBN 0-516-21112-9
    1. Scotland—Juvenile literature. I. Title. II. Series.
  DA762 .S67 2001
  941.1—dc21   00-055569

Acknowledgments

The author wishes to thank the Foreign & Commonwealth office in London and the Scottish Tourist Board in Edinburgh for their assistance in helping him write this book. Mr. Stein and his wife also extend a warm hello to all the friendly Scottish people they met during their wonderful trip to Scotland.

Contents

Cover photo:
A bagpiper

A scene in the
Cheviot Hills

Statue of Robert the Bruce

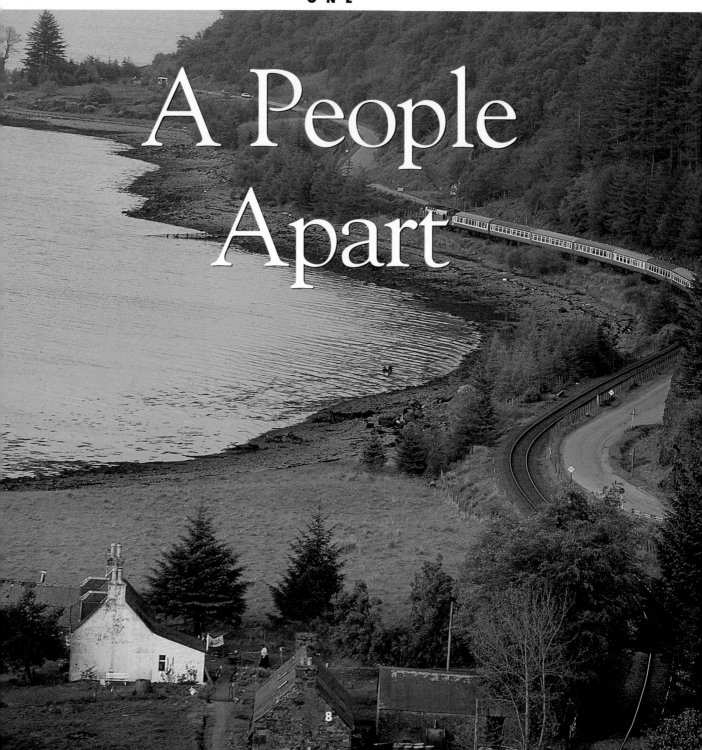

A People Apart

For so long as one hundred remain alive, we will never in any degree be subject to the dominion of the English.
—From the Declaration of Arbroath, 1320

A TRAIN LEAVES LONDON'S KING'S CROSS STATION and heads north. Racing along the track at 110 miles (177 kilometers) per hour, it enters Scotland about three hours later. The train does not stop. No customs inspectors come on board to check passports. To passengers, the border crossing is uneventful. It is as if the train had gone from Illinois to Indiana in the United States. But it is a mistake to think that Scotland is merely a political division of Great Britain. The large island of Great Britain consists of three districts—England, Scotland, and Wales. The Scottish people are British, but they are not English. This is an important distinction. Scots have always considered themselves to be a people apart.

Centuries ago, Scotland was an independent nation whose people spoke languages far different from English. Scotland of old was not a unified country. Rugged mountains lace the north of Scotland. Those

Opposite: **A train passes through the Scottish countryside.**

Mountains surround a valley in Glencoe.

jagged peaks served to separate people into Highlanders and Lowlanders, rival groups that often fought each other. Even the Highlanders were divided into warring bands of families called clans. In 1707, Scotland joined with England to form what became the United Kingdom (U.K.). Before that time, Scotland had a stormy relationship with England.

Today railroads and highways pierce the mountains that were once formidable barriers to travelers. Highlanders and Lowlanders, Scots and the English are enemies no more. Instead the country welcomes tourists. Some 5 million tourists

Boarding a train at Inverness station

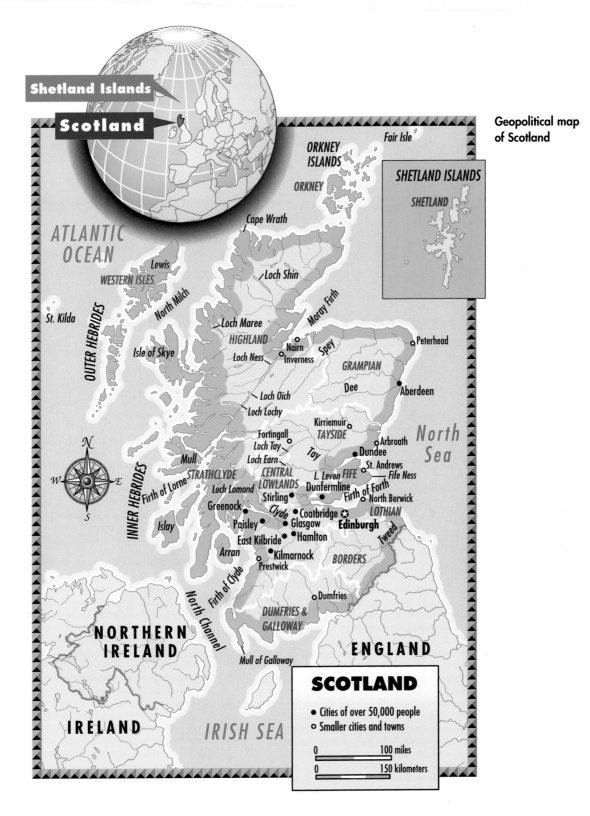

Geopolitical map
of Scotland

Shetland Islands

Scotland

ORKNEY
ISLANDS

Fair Isle

ORKNEY

SHETLAND ISLANDS

SHETLAND

ATLANTIC
OCEAN

Cape Wrath

Lewis

WESTERN ISLES

Loch Shin

North Milch

Loch Maree

Moray Firth

St. Kilda

HIGHLAND

Nairn
Inverness

Spey

GRAMPIAN

Peterhead

Isle of Skye

Loch Ness

OUTER HEBRIDES

Loch Oich

Dee

Aberdeen

Loch Lochy

Kirriemuir

TAYSIDE

Mull

Fortingall
Loch Tay

Loch Earn

Tay

Arbroath

Dundee

St. Andrews

North
Sea

STRATHCLYDE

CENTRAL
LOWLANDS

Firth of Lorne

INNER HEBRIDES

Loch Lomond

L. Leven FIFE
Dunfermline

Fife Ness

Firth of Forth

Islay

Greenock

Stirling

Clyde

North Berwick

Paisley

Coatbridge

Glasgow

☆ Edinburgh

LOTHIAN

Arran

East Kilbride

Hamlton

Kilmarnock
Prestwick

BORDERS

Tweed

North Channel

Firth of Clyde

Dumfries

NORTHERN
IRELAND

DUMFRIES &
GALLOWAY

ENGLAND

Mull of Galloway

IRELAND

IRISH SEA

SCOTLAND

- • Cities of over 50,000 people
- ○ Smaller cities and towns

0   100 miles

0   150 kilometers

come to Scotland each year. Visitors go to Glasgow, Scotland's largest city, and to Edinburgh, its capital. Tourists flock to the seashore, and they travel to the Highlands to see windswept mountain peaks lost in clouds. Modern Scotland holds just over 5 million people, and in many towns tourists outnumber residents during the summer months.

Why is Scotland such a powerful magnet for travelers? Thousands come from North America, New Zealand, Australia, and South Africa seeking their ancestral roots. For centuries, Scots have immigrated to countries scattered about the globe. The United States and Canada were prime destinations for Scots who left their native land long ago. It is estimated that 10 million people of Scottish heritage live in North America. Now Scotland calls its sons and daughters home as the descendants of long-ago immigrants return to capture the spirit of their forebears. Other travelers who have no Scottish heritage quickly learn to love this land and its culture. It is a place of poets, warriors, musicians, and of geniuses in science and invention.

The Scottish people share a unique spirit, a pride in being children of a land that has given so much to the world. This spirit springs to life at Scottish celebrations where men in kilts march to the music of bagpipes and rolling drums. Smiles break out on faces and laughter sounds when the bagpipes explode into the stirring song "Scotland the Brave":

Land of my high endeavor, land of the shining river
Land of my heart forever, Scotland the brave.

A woman bagpiper

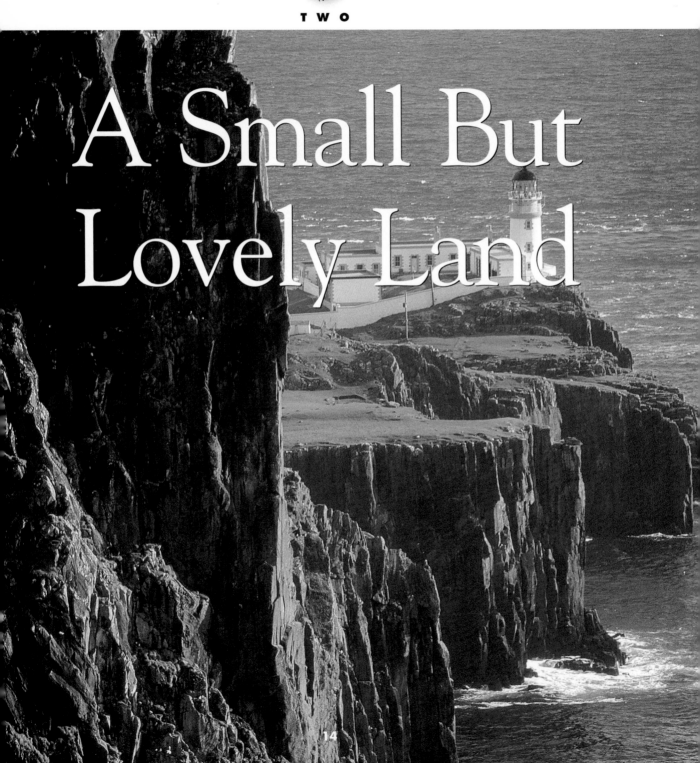

TWO

A Small But Lovely Land

Breathes there a man with soul so dead,
Who never to himself hath said,
This is my own, my native land!
—Sir Walter Scott

A Scot, especially an older one, might say, "Scotland is a wee country, but a bonnie one." Scots enjoy playing with the English language and using their own words—"wee" for *small*; "bonnie" for *pretty*. Wee, Scotland is. It is roughly the size of South Carolina. *Bonnie* is a breezy and musical word, but it fails to fully describe the land's incredible natural beauty. You must visit Scotland to understand why it has inspired such abundant music and poetry.

Scotland lies on the northern third of the island of Great Britain. The island holds three of the four members of the United Kingdom—England, Wales, and Scotland. The other member, Northern Ireland, lies across the Irish Sea just 12 miles (19 km) from Scotland at its closest point.

Scotland's only land neighbor is England, with which it shares a 60-mile (97-km) border. In the southeast that border is marked by the River Tweed. The Cheviot Hills form the Scottish–

Opposite: **A lighthouse on the Isle of Skye**

A view of the Cheviot Hills

English border in the west and south. Many country roads through the Cheviot Hills lack signs announcing the border, so the casual traveler has no idea he or she has crossed from England to Scotland.

In total area, Scotland covers 30,418 square miles (78,783 km). Not counting offshore islands, its greatest distances from north to south are 274 miles (441 km), and 154 miles (248 km) from east to west. These figures make it a tiny land. If Scotland becomes an independent nation, as many Scots wish, it will be one of the smallest countries in Europe.

Scotland is a diverse region where forested mountains stand beside lush green river valleys. Its high country in the north, called the Highlands, is famed for its magnificent mountain scenery. The Lowlands in the south are not really low at all, but instead are made up of chains of hills that run diagonally from sea to sea.

Geologists—men and women who study land forms—divide Scotland into three main land regions. From south to north, those regions are the Southern Uplands, the Central Lowlands, and the Highlands. Land has a way of shaping history and breeding different cultures in particular regions. This is certainly true in Scotland, where the Highlands developed as an almost separate society from the rest of the country.

In the south, along the border with England, rise the Southern Uplands. This region consists of hills that roll over the width of the country like great green waves. One section of the Southern Uplands is called the Borders (after the border with England). Historically, the Southern Uplands were a battleground where armies of English and armies of Scots clashed.

The Central Lowlands is Scotland's "waist," a band that stretches the width of Scotland just below the center of the country. Despite its name, this region too is rippled with hills. Broad river valleys give this area Scotland's richest farmland. Almost three-fourths of Scotland's population live in the Central Lowlands. The two major cities—Glasgow and Edinburgh—are located here, as are many farming and industrial villages.

The Borders region

A variety of vegetation dots the rich soil of the Central Lowlands.

Scotland's Geographical Features

Area: 30,418 square miles (78,783 square kilometers)

Largest City: Glasgow

Highest Elevation: Ben Nevis, 4,406 feet (1,343 meters)

Lowest Elevation: Sea level, along the coast

Greatest Width: 154 miles (248 km)

Narrowest Width: 26 miles (42 km)

Longest Navigable River: Tay River, 120 miles (192 km)

Largest Lake: Loch Lomond, 23 miles (37 km) long and 5 miles (8 km) wide at its widest point

Highest Waterfall in British Isles: Eas-Coul-Aulin

Largest Group of Islands: The Hebrides

Number of Islands off the Coast: Approximately 790

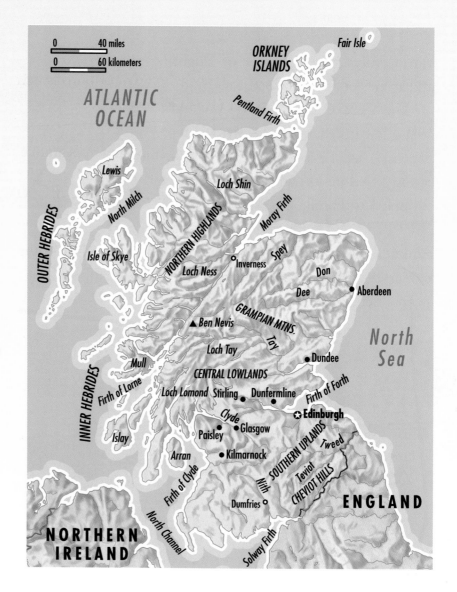

The Highlands spread over the northern two-thirds of the country. Two major mountain ranges—the Grampian Mountains and the Northwest Highlands—dominate this region. The ranges run diagonally northeast to southwest, with the largest mountains rising along the west coast. The tallest mountain (also the highest peak in all of Britain) is Ben Nevis, which stands 4,406 feet (1,343 meters) above sea level. Ben Nevis and its neighboring mountains are made up of sharp cliffs, giving them a rugged and imposing appearance. Certainly, the Highlands have spawned rugged people. Farmland in the region was never productive, and in the old days Highlanders often marched into Lowland farms to raid them of crops and animals. Warfare between Highlanders and their neighbors was a grim way of life.

What's in a Name?

Ben Nevis sounds more like the name of a man than a mountain. But in Scottish usage the word *ben* means "mountain peak," and *Ben Nevis* means "mountain covered by fog." Indeed, the peak of Ben Nevis is often shrouded by thick, pillowlike clouds.

The clouded peak of Ben Nevis dominates this country landscape.

A Scottish Geology Lesson

Scots have their own terms for lakes, hills, forests, and other natural formations. Here is a small sampling:

ben	mountain peak
brae	slope or hill
burn	small stream
firth	an estuary in the sea
glen	valley
inch	meadow or island
loch	lake
moor	a large tract of open land
scree	heaps of stones at the bottom of a hill
strath	a large, flat river valley

Loch Lomond

Lochs, Climate, and the Like

Lakes are called *lochs* (pronounced *locks*). The land is dotted with diamond-clear lochs, most of which are long and narrow and nestled in mountain valleys. Scotland's largest lake is Loch Lomond, which is on the southern edge of the Highlands. Loch Lomond is 23 miles (37 km) long and 5 miles (8 km) wide at its widest point. It is the largest freshwater lake in all of Britain. Most people know the haunting tune and the words of a folk song written to honor Loch Lomond.

Hum it in the morning and the melody stays in your head all day long:

By yon bonnie banks, and by yon bonnie braes
Where the sun shines bright on Loch Lomond
Where me and my true love were ever want to go,
On the bonnie, bonnie banks of Loch Lomond
(Refrain)
Oh, you take the high road, and I'll take the low road
And I'll be in Scotland before you.
But me and my true love will never meet again
On the bonnie, bonnie banks of Loch Lomond.

Loch Ness is one of several lakes on a river and canal system formed at the Great Glen (also called the Glen Mor). The Great Glen is a valley that was created ages ago by earthquakes.

A ferry boat crosses Loch Ness.

In the 1800s, the stream in this valley was widened so that ships could sail between the North Sea and the Atlantic Ocean and avoid Scotland's treacherous coasts. The Great Glen lies between the Grampian Mountains and the Northwest Highlands. Other lakes in the Great Glen are Loch Lochy and Loch Oich. Significant lakes elsewhere in the country include Loch Katrine, which furnishes drinking water for Glasgow, and Loch Earn, which is popular for water sports.

At about 120 miles (192 km) in length, the river Tay is Scotland's largest river. The Tay and its neighbor river to the

Fishing in the misty River Tay

south, the Forth, flow into the North Sea. The river Forth empties into an estuary, or a firth, resulting in a tongue-twisting name—the Firth of Forth. The river Clyde flows into the Atlantic Ocean on Scotland's western shore. The Clyde is an important commercial river because it allows ships to sail into Glasgow. Other major rivers include the Spey, the Dee, and the Tweed.

An abundance of freshwater rivers and lakes is proof that Scotland has more than ample rainfall. Scotland also has dozens of waterfalls, which thunder over mountains. The mountainous west coast gets the most rain. Ben Nevis, which stands near the west coast, is drenched with 150 inches (381 centimeters) of rain or melted snow each year. Lowland Scotland is often subjected to a constant drizzle or a gloomy mist that lasts for days and puts people in a grumpy mood. Scots have a name for long stretches of dreary rain-filled days—the *dreich*. September is usually Scotland's sunniest and driest month.

Edinburgh and Glasgow lie about as far north as Moscow, but they do not suffer the cruel winters typical of that Russian city. Scots can thank the ocean for their mild winter weather. Most of Scotland is warmed by the Gulf Stream, which originates in Mexico and flows thousands of miles to bathe Scotland's shores. January is the coldest month in Edinburgh, when temperatures average a mere 38.6° Fahrenheit (3.7° Celsius). Rarely is Edinburgh or any of Scotland's bigger cities buried by a blizzard.

The Highlands break the pattern of moderate winters. Many Highland mountain slopes are snow covered from October

The Raincoat

A Scotsman named Charles Macintosh (1766–1843) is credited with inventing the raincoat. A chemist born in Glasgow, Macintosh devised many waterproof fabrics. In Great Britain, a raincoat is still called a macintosh.

Looking at Scotland's Cities

The area that is now Glasgow was first settled in the sixth century, when Saint Mungo established a religious community there. Glasgow was created a royal burgh in 1450. Today, it is Scotland's largest city and its commercial and industrial center. The city's places of interest include the cathedral, Provand's Lordship (Glasgow's oldest house, built in 1471), the City Chambers, and the Glasgow Art Gallery and Museum. Approximately 616,430 people live in Glasgow (1996 est.). The city stands at an elevation of 180 feet (54.86 m). The average temperature is 38.3°F (3.5°C) in January and 58.3°F (14.6°C) in July, and average rainfall is 37.4 inches (95.1 cm).

Aberdeen (below) is Scotland's third-largest city, behind Glasgow and Edinburgh. It is an oil-producing giant, but when visiting there don't expect to see a smoky industrial town. Aberdeen is an old city whose major castle dates to the fourteenth century. Most of its downtown buildings were constructed 200 years ago in solid granite. Aberdeen parks and flower gardens have earned it the nickname "The Flower of Scotland." Largely because of the oil industry, city residents enjoy prosperity. About 217,260 people call Aberdeen home. Located at an elevation of 79 feet (24 m), the average temperature is 37.8°F (3.5°C) in January and 56.5°F (13.6°C) in July. Each year, on average, it rains 31 inches (79 cm).

Dundee was established as a Royal Burgh in 1190 and created as a city in 1892. It is Scotland's second-largest industrial center and has long been known for its textiles industries and the production of confectioneries and preserves, particularly marmalade. Due to repeated battles with the English in its early years, few historic buildings have survived to modern times. However, there are some notable architectural features, including the City Churches (three churches under one roof) and Saint Mary's Tower, which dates from the fifteenth century. Dundee's population is about 150,250. The city stands at an elevation of 147 feet (44.8 m) and receives about 31 inches (79 cm) of rain each year.

through May. Hikers in the Highlands must be prepared for sudden and violent weather changes. Blasts of icy winds roaring at 100 miles (16 km) per hour can strike with little warning. Due to its northern location, summer days in Scotland are seldom sweltering. Scots start complaining about the "wretched heat" when temperatures reach 75°F (24°C) in August.

Hikers and hut at the summit of Ben Nevis

By the Sea

Scotland is surrounded on three sides by the sea. Nowhere is more than about 50 miles (80 km) from a seacoast. Scots have always been seafarers. For generations, they have braved the ocean to carry out trade, to catch fish, or to immigrate to far-flung lands.

Scotland's seacoast measures about 2,300 miles (3,700 km), but add in all the inlets and islands and that figure shoots up to more than 6,000 miles (9,656 km) of waterfront. The west coast, where the mountains rise, is far more rugged than the eastern shore. In the east, sandy beaches provide pleasant, if chilly, places to swim.

There are more than 700 islands off Scotland's shores. Many of them are treeless rocks. The islands are clustered in the west and the north. Generally, they are divided into three groups—the Orkney Islands

in the north, the Shetland Islands in the far north, and the Hebrides in the west.

The Shetlands consist of more than 100 islands, but people live on only about 20 of them. These islands, more than a thousand miles from London, are the northernmost territories in all of Great Britain. Long ago, the islands were occupied by Vikings from Scandinavia, and Nordic customs and languages still survive on the isolated Shetlands.

A view of the east coast of Mainland, one of the Shetland Islands

Northern Twilight

The Shetland Islands are as far north as Alaska. As in Alaska, the sun hangs above the horizon as if it is refusing to set during the summer. In June, the Shetlands have sunlight twenty-three hours a day. At about midnight, the sun finally dips below the horizon. Islanders call that one hour of twilight the "simmer dim."

Below the Shetlands stand the Orkney Islands. There are 67 islands in this group, and fewer than 30 of them are inhabited. George Mackay Brown, a poet who lived on the islands, claimed the Orkneys spread out to the sea "like the backs of sleeping whales." Islanders earn their livings through farming, fishing, and tourism. In the summer, tourists arrive by ferryboat and take long walks along the Orkneys' breathtaking cliffs.

Rocky cliffs of the Orkney Islands

The largest group of islands off Scotland's coast is the Hebrides. Some 500 islands make up the Hebrides, but many of them are mere outcroppings in the water. The Hebrides are separated into two groups—the Outer Hebrides and the Inner Hebrides. The Inner Hebrides are closer to the coast. The primary island of the Inner Hebrides, the Isle of Skye, is connected to the mainland by a bridge. All the other Scottish islands are reachable only by boat or airplane.

It is impossible to separate poetry and music from the land of Scotland. The two are married forever, and it is a happy union. The country's most beloved poet and creator of songs is Robert Burns (1759–1796). Many of Burn's works hail the natural world of his native Scotland:

The wanton coot the water skims,
Among the reeds the ducklings cry,
The stately swan majestic swims,
And ev'ry thing is blest but I.

The Skye Bridge, connecting the Isle of Skye to the mainland

Nature's Gifts

An OLD BALLAD TELLS OF A HOMESICK SCOTTISH soldier who is stationed on foreign soil. The soldier takes long, lonely walks. The words of the song say, "He traveled far away and soldiered far away." However, the troubled soldier can find no satisfaction in the countryside. Always, the Scotsman says of the foreign hills, "They are not the hills of home."

Opposite: **Meadow flowers in the Highlands**

Scotland's Green Hills

In ancient times, dense forests covered most of Scotland. Those woodlands were chopped down long ago to clear fields for farms and pastures. Constant warfare in the Highlands led to destructive forest fires, which also stripped the region of

John Muir, Naturalist

One of the world's greatest advocates of conservation was born in the Scottish town of Dunbar. John Muir (1838–1814) moved to the United States with his family when he was eleven. As a young man, he traveled west seeking "anywhere that is wild" and hiked into California's spectacular Yosemite Valley. He later persuaded the U.S. Congress to establish Yosemite National Park. Through Muir's efforts, hundreds of millions of acres of wilderness in the United States became protected conservation areas.

North of Loch Tay is a tiny village called Fortingall. Villagers there point with pride to a twisted yew tree that scientists judge to be about 3,000 years old. According to village residents, it is the oldest living tree in all of Europe.

Digging peat moss on the Isle of Islay

trees. Today, only about 15 percent of Scotland is forested. Patches of thick trees are found in the Southern Uplands and in the Highlands. Typical trees include Scots pine, Norwegian spruce, Douglas fir, and larch.

Peat moss thrives in areas where rainwater tends to gather rather than run off. The moss grows in layers with live plants resting on beds of dead plants. Many of Scotland's islands are covered with peat moss. Islanders pick the moss, allow it to dry, and then burn it as fuel in the winter months.

A bouquet of yellow saxifrage and purple heather on a rocky Highland trail

Mountains give rise to a brilliant array of shrubs and plants. Purple heather, a favorite plant of Scots, blankets mountain slopes. In bloom, the plant produces heather bells, which look like tiny bells. Heather bells are mentioned in Scottish folk songs. Azalea, dwarf willow, and saxifrages also grow on high mountains. Delicate white flowers, called avens, bloom on ledges where they are out of reach of deer and sheep.

Queen Elizabeth Forest Park

Scotland has forty Natural Scenic Areas, places where nature is protected by law. One of the most popular of these conservation sites is the Queen Elizabeth Forest Park, which spreads over 41,600 acres (16,842 hectares) near Loch Lomond. Animals in the park include red deer and wild goats. The park is named for Britain's Queen Elizabeth II (1926–), a well-known lover of nature.

Many nature lovers claim the slopes of Ben Lawers, which rises above Loch Tay, have the most fascinating variety of wild plants in the country.

In the spring, meadows explode with wildflowers—hyacinth, meadowsweet, meadow buttercup, and various wild roses. Scots have a song honoring just about every occasion or activity. In one ballad a young man invites his girlfriend to pick wild mountain thyme, a delicious spice that grows on hillsides:

And we'll all go together
To pick wild mountain thyme.
All along the bloomin' valley,
Will you go, lassie, go.

Animals in the Wild

Scotland is home to an estimated quarter-million red deer. Long admired for their grace and beauty, red deer seem to defy gravity as they bound about their forest homes. Herds of red

deer, sometimes 100 strong, graze by roadsides or in meadows. Red deer are the largest of Scotland's wild animals. Rabbits and squirrels are found everywhere. Foxes abound, but they are seldom seen. Rarest of the wild mammals is the wildcat, which lives in remote areas.

Red deer

A European wildcat

The National Trust for Scotland

Many wilderness areas are preserved with the help of an organization called the National Trust for Scotland. Established in 1931, the organization is a charity, not a government agency. It has 230,000 members and administers more than 180,000 acres of land. The National Trust also cares for castles, historic houses, and birthplaces of famous Scots. The group's goal is to preserve Scottish treasures for future generations.

Birds fly in thick, noisy formations over the coast. Coastal birds include eider duck and geese. Some offshore islands are called "bird islands," because their only inhabitants are seabirds. The Orkney Islands are the nesting place for millions of winged creatures. Bird colonies there are the thickest in all of Europe. Common birds on the Orkneys are the hen harrier, the short-eared owl, and the red-throated diver.

Saint Kilda Island in the Shetland group tells an interesting back-to-nature story. The island is a rugged place whose sea-washed cliffs are the highest in all of Britain. For hundreds of years, a small group of hardy people lived there and worked at fishing, tending sheep, and catching seabirds. In 1930, the last thirty-six residents of the island asked the government to relocate them. No permanent colony of people ever returned to Saint Kilda. Now the island is the nesting place for huge

The Miserable Midge

Scotland is a paradise for walking, but a tiny biting fly called the midge often takes the fun out of outdoor adventures. No bigger than a North American gnat, the midge torments rural people in the summer months. It is most aggressive in the early morning and at sundown. You can try repellents, or you can cover your face with a special "midge net." Most of the time, though, all you can do is swat at these pests, which buzz in your ears and sting your face. They are called the "Scourge of Scotland."

flocks of birds including the Saint Kilda wren, a bird that is unique to the island. Some 1,400 wild sheep, leftovers from the time of human habitation, roam the island's grasslands. The birds and sheep don't seem to miss people one bit.

The largest of Scotland's birds is the gannet, a seabird whose wingspan can measure 6 feet (1.8 m) from tip to tip. An interesting inland bird is the ptarmigan (pronounced with a silent "p"). As camouflage, the ptarmigan changes its colors with the seasons, from gray in the summer to pure white in the winter. A lucky bird-watcher might spot a golden eagle soaring over the Highlands or the Hebrides Islands. An estimated 300 golden eagles nest in Scotland.

Marine life thrives along Scotland's coast. Fishers bring in shrimps, crab, lobster, halibut, and herring, although the catch has decreased in recent years due to overfishing. Schools of porpoises dart in and out of the coastal waters. Whales can also be observed from shore. Seals live on the islands and in many firths. Inland waters hold salmon and trout. Now and then, hikers will spot otters scurrying around riverbanks.

A golden eagle

Grey seals on the Isle of Skye

The Loch Ness Monster

Scotland's most famous animal (or its best-known myth) is the Loch Ness Monster. Does it really live in the depths of Loch Ness, or is the monster simply a product of the Scots' celebrated storytelling art? Reports of such an animal date back many years. In the 1500s, a man wrote, "A terrible beast issued out of the water [at Loch Ness] early one morning about midsummer and knocked down trees and killed three men with its tail." People who have seen it claim the monster is green or yellow, has two humps on its back, a long neck, and an enormous tail.

Thousands of years ago, the loch was an inland sea, and some people argue it is possible that relatives of the dinosaurs might have survived here. Because Loch Ness is the deepest lake in Scotland, such creatures could hide in its murky bottom. Today, the Loch Ness Monster is one of Scotland's greatest tourist attractions. Get off the train at Inverness, and a person dressed in a playful-looking monster costume offers guided tours of Loch Ness. No one is afraid of the monster. It is affectionately called "Nessie."

Scottish-bred Animals

Along the country roads of Scotland are flocks of sheep so thick they cover hills like rolling snow. Most are Blackface sheep, which have a grayish-white coat and a black "mask" on their faces. Blackface sheep, also called Scottish blackface, were bred long ago in the Scottish highlands. They are one of many animals developed by Scot farmers and ranchers.

A shepherd guides his sheep along a road in the Outer Hebrides.

A Shetland pony and its young

The Shetland pony is a cute little horse that measures only about 3 feet (90 cm) high. Shetland ponies originated in the Shetland Islands. They were once used to pull carts in coal mines because they were strong despite their small size. In modern times, Shetlands have been cultivated as pets and mounts for small children. Tiny kids can ride on their backs and still be close to the ground if they fall.

By contrast, the Scots also developed the Clydesdale, one of the largest horse breeds. On television, you can see teams of Clydesdales pulling wagons loaded with beer barrels.

Scots have produced several forms of beef cattle—the Galloway, the Highland, and the Aberdeen-Angus. Shaggy

Tandem Clydesdales pulling a plow

Highland cattle graze in rugged mountain glens. These huge beasts with long horns look like an American bison except they are ginger in color. Aberdeen-Angus cattle are noted for their tasty meat.

The country's best-known breed of dog is the Scottish terrier, or Scottie. The friendly Scottie is a small dog that was first raised in the Highlands in the 1800s. Sheep herding would be impossible without the assistance of sheepdogs. Collies were bred in Scotland in the 1600s and have been partners with sheep ranchers ever since. The Border collie is native to the Borders region, while the Shetland collie comes from the Shetland Islands.

Highland cattle

Greyfriars Bobby

Greyfriars Bobby was a mixed-breed terrier owned and loved by a police officer in Edinburgh. In 1858, the police officer died and was buried in the Greyfriars churchyard. His dog, Bobby, stood over his grave refusing to move. For the next fourteen years, until his death, Bobby maintained a vigil at the gravesite. Sympathetic townspeople fed him and gave him a collar so he wouldn't be picked up as a stray. A statue of Greyfriars Bobby now stands near the gravesite, and his collar is displayed at a local museum.

Scotland the Brave

Scots, who have with Wallace bled,
Scots, whom Bruce have often led;
Welcome to your gory bed,
Or to victory!

THOSE LINES, WHICH HAVE BEEN SLIGHTLY TRANSLATED from the Scottish dialect, are from a poem written in the late 1700s by Scotland's national poet, Robert Burns. The poem describes a terrible battle that pitted Scot soldiers against a mighty English army. Scottish history, sadly, is filled with episodes of war and bloodshed. But the country's past is also the story of a people to whom freedom is as important as life.

Opposite: **A statue of Robert the Bruce at Stirling Castle**

The First Scots

Scotland has been inhabited for about 8,000 years. Its first residents came from the European mainland and southern England. The earliest inhabitants made tools out of flint and constructed circular houses from stones. Bronze came to the British Isles about 5,000 years ago. The new metal was used to make axes, knives, swords, and decorative statues. One group of people who lived in Scotland, called the Beaker Folk, buried their dead with pottery cups.

About 500 B.C., the Celts came from Europe and introduced horses, plows, and new crops to the British Isles. They also brought iron, a metal far stronger than bronze. Using iron

The Brochs

The Celts built stone towers, called *brochs*, to serve as watchtowers to help protect their settlements. More than 500 of these ancient brochs are scattered about Scotland. The best-preserved broch stands on the small island of Mousa in the Shetlands.

Ancient Monuments

Near the small town of Stromness on the Orkney Islands are the ruins of a farming and fishing village that was inhabited some 4,000 to 4,500 years ago. Called Skara Brae, this remarkably well-preserved site is made up of six tiny houses and what appears to be a workshop. Inside the houses are stone slabs that were covered with grass and used as beds.

Another ancient monument in the Orkney Islands is the Ring of Brodgar. This circle of thirty-six stones (originally there were sixty) is similar to a more famous structure, Stonehenge, in England. It is believed people used stone rings for worship or to calculate movements of the sun. The Ring of Brodgar, which dates from 1560 B.C., is the largest circle of stones in Scotland. One of its stones stands 15 feet tall and weighs several tons.

swords, the Celts vanquished the people of Britain. Winston Churchill, a British statesman and historian, put their conquest simply when he wrote, "Men armed with iron entered Britain and killed the men of bronze."

In A.D. 43, the Romans sailed from Europe and began a slow occupation of the British Isles. In Scotland, the Romans and the northern Celts fought bitter battles. Roman soldiers called the Celts a primitive and barbaric people. Said one Roman writer, "They live in huts, go naked and unshod. They can bear hunger and cold and all manner of hardship. [When attacked,] they will retire into their marshes and hold out for days with only their heads above water." The northerners also painted their faces to terrify opponents in war. The Romans called them Picts, from the Latin word *picti*, meaning "painted."

Hoping to protect themselves from the warlike Picts, the Romans built a great wall across northern England in the 120s. It was named Hadrian's Wall, after the Roman emperor who approved of its construction. The power of Rome declined due to struggles at home, and in the 400s, Roman forces left Britain. But Hadrian's Wall remained, serving as a boundary of sorts between England and Scotland. Even then, almost 1,600 years ago, the wall signified that the Scots were a people apart.

Visiting Hadrian's Wall

Long ago, Hadrian's Wall ran 73 miles (117 km) from coast to coast and was manned by 20,000 soldiers. It stood more than 20 feet (6 m) high and was thick enough to allow two people to walk side by side along its top. Portions of Hadrian's Wall still stand today. The wall is in England, slightly south of the present-day Scottish border.

A view of Hadrian's Wall

A Kingdom Takes Shape

Near the year 500, a Celtic tribe left Ireland and established a territory on Scotland's west coast. The Romans knew of these people before they migrated and called them the Scotti. The Scotti (or Scot) band grew in numbers and in power. In 843, Kenneth MacAlpin, king of the Scots, absorbed the Picts into his kingdom. By 1034, much of the northern British Isles was under control of the Scots.

Christianity gradually spread through most of the kingdom. The leading Christian monk was Saint Columba, who came to Scotland from Ireland in 563. Before Columba's arrival, the Pict and Scot peoples worshipped pagan gods. Columba converted them carefully, without insulting their old practices. He built churches on top of sacred hills that had long been places of worship. Saint Columba laid the groundwork for

St. Columba preaches to the people.

future Christian ministers. Roman Catholic priests arrived next, and Catholicism became the strongest religion in Scotland.

Vikings from Scandinavia landed on the northern islands in the 800s and established permanent villages there. Bands also came from England and settled in the fertile Central Lowlands region. The influx of people led to different languages. In the northern islands, the languages of Norway and Denmark prevailed. The royalty and the upper classes spoke Scottish Gaelic, a dialect of the Gaelic language of Ireland. In the south, people spoke Anglo-Saxon, which is the root of modern English.

Warfare was the scourge of early Scotland. The death of a Scottish king often triggered a war as rivals fought for the vacant throne. In 1040, a general named Macbeth killed King Duncan in battle

Map labels:
ATLANTIC OCEAN
Shetland Is.
PICTS
SCOTS
NORTH SEA
Inchtuthil
BRITONS
ANGLES
Hadrian's Wall 117–138
IRISH
Stanwick

Viking Scotland, 10th Century

☐ Viking settlement

Shakespeare's Macbeth

The English playwright William Shakespeare (1564–1616) wrote a distorted version of the Macbeth story. In Shakespeare's rendition, General Macbeth murdered King Duncan while he was asleep. Shakespeare portrayed Macbeth as a man so crazed by ambition that he lost interest in life itself. Macbeth asks, "What is life?" He concludes, poetically, "[Life] is a tale told by an idiot, full of sound and fury, Signifying nothing."

and became king of Scotland. Seventeen years later, Malcolm III, the son of Duncan, avenged his father's death by murdering Macbeth. Malcolm III was married to an Englishwoman, and he admired the English way of life. However, in 1093, Malcolm III was killed in battle against an English army.

The Time of Heroes

To the south, English kings attempted to expand their territory, and Scotland became a victim of England's hunger for land. Scotland had only one-fifth the population of England, and its best farmland was near the border and subject to English occupation. Yet, rallying behind military leaders, the Scottish people fought for their independence. The wars of independence against England were bloody affairs, but Scot patriots look back at the era and remember a time of heroes.

Macbeth, King of Scotland

The Wallace Monument

At Stirling stands a 220-foot (67-m) tower called the Wallace Monument. Visitors are invited to climb a 246-step spiral staircase to the top of the tower and view the Stirling Battleground. At the top, enclosed in glass, is Wallace's sword. The sword was made especially for him and measures 5 feet 6 inches (168 cm) from handle to tip. In Wallace's era a man 5 feet 5 inches (165 cm) in height was considered tall. This means that Wallace, a giant in his times, led his troops into battle wielding a sword that was taller than most of his opponents.

One hero was William Wallace (1272?–1305). We know of his exploits largely through the words of a poet named Blind Harry, who lived 170 years after Wallace's death. Wallace was a muscular man who some scholars believe stood seven feet tall. When he was about twenty-five, he killed an English sheriff because—according to Blind Harry's poem—the sheriff had murdered Wallace's wife-to-be. Wallace then commanded a rebel band that clashed with English armies. His greatest victory came at the town of Stirling, where he led a ragtag force of spearmen to victory against powerful English cavalry.

William Wallace is one of Scotland's most enduring heroes.

Villains reigned during the time of heroes. One villain, in the opinion of Scot historians, was the English king Edward I (1239–1307). His hatred for the Scottish people was so intense he earned the nickname the Hammer of the Scots. In 1298, Edward I led his army to battle against William Wallace at the town of Falkirk. The Scots were hopelessly outnumbered. English archers, who had mastered the use of the longbow, showered Wallace's men with arrows. Then the English cavalry swarmed into the battered Scot formations. Perhaps the fortunes of battle could have been reversed if the Scot cavalry had joined the fray. But Scot horse soldiers were

The Stone of Destiny

For centuries, a gray block of sandstone rested in an honored place at the abbey in the town of Scone. It was believed the prophet Jacob used the stone as a pillow when he dreamed of angels ascending to heaven. Every Scot king traveled to Scone to sit on this revered rock for the coronation ceremony officially making him lord of the land. It was called the Stone of Destiny or the Stone of Scone. In 1296, Edward I raided the abbey at Scone and made off with the precious relic. He moved the Stone of Destiny to Westminster Abbey, in London, where it remained for the next 700 years.

commanded by noblemen who feared Wallace because of his close ties with the peasants. The noblemen on horseback did little to stop the slaughter.

Wallace escaped death at Falkirk, but seven years later he was captured by the English and put on trial. The rebel leader was sentenced to a terrible execution. He was hung, cut open while still alive, and finally his body was chopped into four parts, which were scattered over the British Isles.

Braveheart

The story of William Wallace was told in the epic 1995 film *Braveheart*, starring Mel Gibson (right). The movie's script was loose with historic facts. For example, Wallace was about twenty years old when his father was hanged by the English, not eight as the movie suggests. Nevertheless, the film was a smashing success. *Braveheart* won five Academy Awards, including Best Picture and Best Director. Before the movie, Wallace was little known outside of Scotland. The film made him a folk hero around the world.

Enter another Scot hero, Robert the Bruce (1274–1329). In 1306, he was crowned king of Scotland, but the English refused to recognize his leadership. Bruce lived in exile and gradually gathered an army. In 1314, he fought the English at the Battle of Bannockburn. The English army was led by Edward II, son of the Hammer of the Scots. This time the Scots—noblemen as well as peasants—were united. Robert the Bruce inflicted a crushing defeat on the English army, and Edward II was forced to recognize Scottish independence.

Bruce and the Spider

A story holds that Robert the Bruce, while hiding from the English, spent a night in a miserable country shack. There he watched a spider dangling from its web on the ceiling, attempting to swing from one beam to another. Six times it tried, and six times it failed. Bruce concluded that if this lowly spider could struggle so bravely to complete its task, then he too must continue his fight against England. Once more the spider swung, and it succeeded on its seventh try. Thus Robert the Bruce was inspired to lead his country to independence.

Robert the Bruce leads his troops at the Battle of Bannockburn.

In 1320, Scot noblemen assembled in the town of Arbroath, where they wrote the Declaration of Arbroath and submitted it to the pope in Rome. In bold and forceful words, it said that Scotland was an independent nation. The declaration read, in part, "For so long as one hundred of us remain alive, we will never in any degree be subject to the dominion of the English. . . . For it is not honor, nor riches, nor glory that we fight for, but for liberty alone."

Reformation and Union

Independence did not bring peace to Scotland. The English continued to wage a series of wars. Seeking allies, Scot kings made alliances with France, England's traditional enemy. The ties with France sometimes did Scotland more harm than good. In 1503, the Scot king James IV married an English

A depiction of the ill-fated battle at Flodden Field

princess, Margaret Tudor. It was hoped the marriage would promote peace between Scotland and England. But France urged James to go to war against England. James led his troops into battle at Flodden Field in 1513, and Scotland suffered the worst defeat in its history. Some 10,000 Scot soldiers lost their lives at Flodden, including King James IV. One report said the king died on the battlefield "riddled with arrows."

Independence also failed to bring unity to Scotland. The Highlands had long been a troubled region ruled by feuding groups of families called clans. The clans were known, and feared, by the name of their chiefs—Clan MacGregor, Clan MacDonald, Clan Campbell, and so on. Mostly the clans battled one another, but they sometimes joined forces and stormed from the mountains to raid Lowland villages of cattle and gold. Lowlanders learned to hate the Highlanders with greater passion than they hated the English. Stories circulated claiming that Highlanders weren't even human. Some Londoners believed that men of the Scottish Highlands had tails attached to their bottoms. A Lowland poet once wrote a long stanza in which he compared Highlanders to horse manure.

The roar of battle almost never ceased over Scotland between 1300 and 1700. Yet amazingly, artistic and intellectual life flourished. Castles and churches were built. Wealthy landowners erected mansions surrounded with statues and works of art. Learning expanded. Saint Andrews College, in the town of Saint Andrews, was founded in 1412. Aberdeen University was founded in 1495. A medical college was established at Edinburgh in 1507. Poet John Barbour (1320–1395) wrote heroic poems praising the nation's hero, Robert the Bruce. Another poet, Gavin Douglas (1474–1522), studied at Saint Andrews College and rose to high office in the church.

In 1517, Martin Luther, a monk in Germany, nailed a piece of paper to the door of a Catholic church. The paper contained demands that the church change, or *reform*, old practices. Luther thereby launched a movement called the Reformation. In the next forty years, half the people of Europe shifted their loyalties from Catholicism to various Protestant faiths.

In Scotland, the Reformation was led by a one-time priest named John Knox (1515?–1572). During Knox's youth, the Catholic Church owned much of the land and wealth in Scotland. Knox once saw a friend burned at the stake for defying church authority. A fiery speaker, Knox moved crowds into riot as he marched about the country denouncing the church and its practices. Charged with religious frenzy, mobs burned churches and tore down ancient abbeys.

Into this turmoil stepped the very beautiful and passionate Mary, Queen of Scots (1542–1587). She became queen of Scotland when she was a week old and her father, King James V, died. Mary

Gifted speaker John Knox addresses Mary, Queen of Scots.

Mary's Heroic Escape

In 1567, Mary, Queen of Scots was imprisoned in a tower on Castle Island in the middle of Loch Leven. Mary charmed a teenage boy who lived on the grounds. One night the boy stole the keys to her chamber, rowed the queen ashore, and then defiantly threw the keys into the lake. This daring escape is no idle story. Three hundred years later, divers found the chamber keys on the lake's bottom.

had a weak husband and at least two lovers. One lover was murdered, then her husband was murdered, and she finally married the last of her lovers. Mary was a Catholic at a time when her country was undergoing the bloody change from Catholicism to Protestantism. Protestant pressure forced Mary to give up the throne of Scotland. In desperation, she fled to London to seek help from her cousin, Queen Elizabeth. This was a fatal mistake. Elizabeth feared Mary would win followers in England, and she had Mary beheaded.

By the 1560s, the Scottish Reformation was over. The Presbyterian Church was now the national church of Scotland. The time was ripe for a very unusual development. In 1603, Queen Elizabeth of England died. Before her death, she named King James VI (1566–1625) of Scotland to be her heir. He was the son of Mary, Queen of Scots, who Elizabeth had ordered beheaded. What sort of folly was this? Why should

A portrait of King James VI of Scotland (James I of England)

Elizabeth pick a sitting king of Scotland to be England's king? Times had changed. England and Scotland were by this time both Protestant countries. James was a Protestant king. Both sides had grown weary of the warfare that had raged on and off for 300 years. James went to London and became king of both England and Scotland. The two countries remained separate; they simply had the same king. This unusual arrangement was called the Personal Union.

Civil war broke out in England in 1642 as Englishmen who supported the English Parliament battled those who supported the king. Scotland was drawn into this civil war. Meanwhile, the power of Scotland's own Parliament (the government apart from the king) grew. In 1707, the English and the Scottish Parliaments met and passed the Act of Union. This historic act created the United Kingdom by bringing England, Scotland, and Wales under one government. (Northern Ireland joined the United Kingdom much later.) From the point of view of history, the sudden oneness was a miracle. Scotland and England—the forever feuding neighbors—had kissed, made up, and gotten married. Theirs was not always a happy marriage. But it was a marriage that lasted almost 300 years.

Problems of Union

In the 1500s, Spain, Portugal, France, England, and other nations sent ships into unknown waters and established colonies in far-flung lands. England's colonial network grew to include one quarter of the world's land and embraced one-quarter of its people. The Scots were partners with the English

The Scotch-Irish

In the 1600s, thousands of Scot Protestants went to Ireland seeking religious freedom. After a few decades, they determined Ireland was still too close to meddling government officials in the old country. So they moved to the Thirteen Colonies, where they boldly settled the western frontier. Called the Scotch-Irish, they built log cabins and carved out farms in the wilderness states of Tennessee, Kentucky, and Ohio. Scotch-Irish were among General George Washington's most trusted soldiers in the Revolutionary War (1775–1783).

in this empire-building process. North America was the great magnet that drew in Scot pioneers. So many Scots went to Canada that the province of Nova Scotia (Latin for "New Scotland") was named in their honor. Between 1715 and 1775, some 250,000 Scots arrived at the land which became the United States.

The Act of Union embittered many Scots, especially the Highlanders. Highland clans rallied around James Edward Stuart (1688–1766), the man they recognized as king. The Highland rebels were called the Jacobites. In 1715, the Jacobite Rebellion broke out. The rebellion did not strictly pit the Scots against the English. Instead, the British government stood against the rebels, most of whom were Highlanders. The first victory went to the government, as troops defeated the Jacobites and James Edward Stuart fled to France.

Rob Roy

A celebrated Highlander was Rob Roy McGregor (1671–1734). Was he a hero, or was he a bandit? Indeed, Rob Roy was a cattle rustler. But Sir Walter Scott, who in 1818 wrote the romantic novel *Rob Roy*, claimed Rob Roy was forced into the outlaw life after a powerful landowner cheated him out of money. Moreover, he had the image of a Robin Hood, a man who plundered the rich but fed the poor. The popular 1995 movie *Rob Roy* also presented him as a champion of honorable causes.

Young Charles Edward Stuart, "Bonnie Prince Charlie"

A second Jacobite Rebellion began in 1745, this time led by James's son Charles Edward Stuart (1720–1788). He was called "Bonnie Prince Charlie" and the "Young Pretender," the youthful and handsome hero of poems and folk songs. Bonnie Prince Charlie gathered an army of 5,000 fanatical Highlanders and won early battles against government forces. The rebels even took over Edinburgh, Scotland's capital. But in 1746, a huge army commanded by the Duke of Cumberland met Charles at Culloden Moor near Inverness. The result was a slaughter for the Highland army. More than 1,200 Highlanders were killed. The Duke of Cumberland put to death many wounded survivors of the battle.

Bonnie Prince Charlie escaped death. With the help of a friend, Flora MacDonald, he dressed in women's clothing and disguised himself as an English maid. He then sailed to the Isle of Skye and later went to France. Charles lived the rest of his life as an alcoholic, who complained that the Highlanders failed him at his time of greatest need. Yet Bonnie Prince Charlie possessed a special charm that warmed the hearts of the Scottish people. A lovely song tells of his flight to the Isle of Skye:

> *Speed bonnie boat like a bird on the wing.*
> *Onward the sailors cry;*
> *Carry the lad that's born to be king*
> *Over the sea to Skye.*

The disaster at Culloden ended the old Highlander way of life. Government troops stormed through the Highlands burning villages, looting farms, and hanging clan chiefs. An occupying army remained in the Highlands for years to come. Culloden Moor was also the last major battle fought on British soil. Scotland was now solidly part of Great Britain. The ancient and once independent land was ruled from London. England and Scotland faced the future together, and their histories became largely intertwined.

Industrialization

In the 1750s, a young Scotsman worked as an instrument maker for

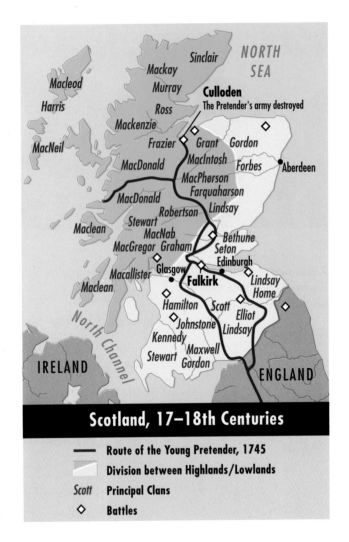

Scotland, 17–18th Centuries

— Route of the Young Pretender, 1745
Division between Highlands/Lowlands
Scott Principal Clans
◇ Battles

A depiction of Scottish inventor James Watt with his early steam engine

the University of Glasgow. The job was a perfect match for his skills because he delighted in tinkering with mechanical devices. He was James Watt (1736–1819), and he helped to change the world. Remember Watt every time you screw in a lightbulb of 75 watts, 100 watts, or whatever. The *watt* is a unit of electric power, and the term is named after the brilliant Scottish inventor. Steam-powered machinery was not new in Watt's time. But existing steam engines required enormous amounts of coal to produce very little power. Watt built a vastly improved steam-driven motor, and he invented a crank system that allowed the motor to turn wheels. Following Watt's model, other inventors designed steam-powered ships, train engines, and machines for factories. This machinery propelled humankind into a new era called the Industrial Revolution.

Scotland's first major industry was the manufacture of textiles, or cloth products. Textile factories began with machinery driven by waterwheels built over swift-running rivers. Steam-driven machinery made the textile industry more efficient. One industry led to others. Steam required coal as fuel. Scotland was rich in coal, and coal mining boomed. Iron made up the bones of the Industrial Revolution. A huge foundry called the Carron Ironworks was built near Falkirk in the 1760s. The city of Glasgow became an industrial giant as its factories churned out textiles and its shipyards built huge vessels.

The Industrial Revolution brought people from the farms to the cities. Glasgow's population jumped tenfold from 1740 to 1840. The greatest change took place in the Highlands, where a population drain called the Highland Clearances occurred during the early 1800s. With the textile industry expanding, Highland landowners found sheep to be more profitable than traditional crops. Consequently, the powerful landowners, many of them former clan chiefs, forced peasant farmers off their land. The peasants drifted to the cities or emigrated to the United States. Most of the farmers eventually found a better life, but the Highland Clearances remain the saddest story of Scotland's Industrial Revolution.

Industrialization created a huge gulf between rich and poor. The factory-working class lived in wretched slums in Glasgow, Falkirk, Edinburgh, Dundee, Aberdeen, and other cities. Coal mines employed children as young as six to crawl into tiny shafts and chip away at coal. The nimble fingers of women ran the textile machines in dark and airless factories. Factory owners reasoned they could pay women less than men because women workers were unwelcome in shops other than the textile factories.

A reform movement took hold in Scotland and the rest of Great Britain during the grimmest days of the Industrial Revolution. Labor unions in the United Kingdom forced the government to sign the Factory Act in 1838, which restricted child labor. Early in the 1800s, voting for Parliament was restricted to property owners only. Gradually, voting privileges were extended to all men, but women could not vote until the 1920s. One of the greatest triumphs of the reformers was the Education Act of 1872, which required all children aged five through thirteen to attend school.

Women at work in a gloomy cotton mill

A bombed tenement building at Clydeside, World War II

Devolution

Through most of the 1900s, Scotland's history paralleled that of the United Kingdom. When the United Kingdom went to war, so did Scotland. In World War I (1914–1918), some 80,000 Scots died in the bloody trenches of France. During World War II (1939–1945), German aircraft rained bombs on Scottish shipyard cities, killing hundreds of civilians. Sandwiched between the wars was the Great Depression of the 1930s, in which Scots suffered terrible unemployment and poverty. In each of these events, Scotland bore the pain and celebrated the triumphs equally with the other members of the United Kingdom.

But toward the end of the twentieth century, the United Kingdom became less united. A new movement—toward Devolution—began. Devolution meant home rule for

Scotland and Wales. It was the opposite of revolution, which implied a violent struggle to achieve political aims. Instead, Devolution came about gradually, peacefully, and with the consent of all parties.

When and why did Devolution begin? For years, many Scots believed the British government treated them like poor country cousins. After World War II, England enjoyed economic recovery while much of Scotland was impoverished. Also, the Scots consider themselves to be a people apart from the English. Their customs, religion, accent, and history are different from those of their southern neighbors. Still, few Scots talked of independence. A political party called the Scottish National Party (SNP) was formed in 1928 and called for separation from the United Kingdom. The SNP never won an election. Its members were dismissed as romantic dreamers. Then the impossible happened. In a 1967 election, the Clyde Valley town of Hamilton sent an SNP delegate to Parliament in London. Tiny Hamilton started a dizzying political movement. In 1974, the SNP won more than 800,000 votes and had eleven delegates in Parliament.

Most people advocating Devolution did not favor a complete break with the United Kingdom. Instead, they hoped to achieve some form of home rule, or self-government, for Scotland. Devolution suffered a setback in a 1979 referendum when only 33 percent of the Scottish people voted for home rule. But the sentiment for home rule remained. Two major political parties—the Labour Party and the Conservative Party—dominate British politics. In nationwide elections,

Return of the Stone of Destiny

On Saint Andrews Day, November 30, 1996, a group of dignitaries marched to Westminster Abbey in London. Bands played somber music. With great pomp and pageantry, the dignitaries moved the revered Stone of Destiny from Westminster Abbey, where it had sat for 700 years, and put it on a special truck for return to Scotland. This is the stone that Edward I, the Hammer of the Scots, had confiscated from the abbey at Scone in 1296. The Stone of Destiny, or Stone of Scone, now rests in an honored spot in Edinburgh Castle.

Scot voters generally prefer the Labour Party, and the Labourites helped keep Devolution alive. A new election was held in 1997, and this time three out of every four Scots chose to establish a separate parliament. Devolution was now a fact.

Devolution did not mean independence—not yet, anyway. It simply gave Scotland a greater voice over its own affairs. What Devolution will mean in the future is a matter of debate for the new Scottish government.

Voters celebrate the 1997 election of a separate Scottish Parliament.

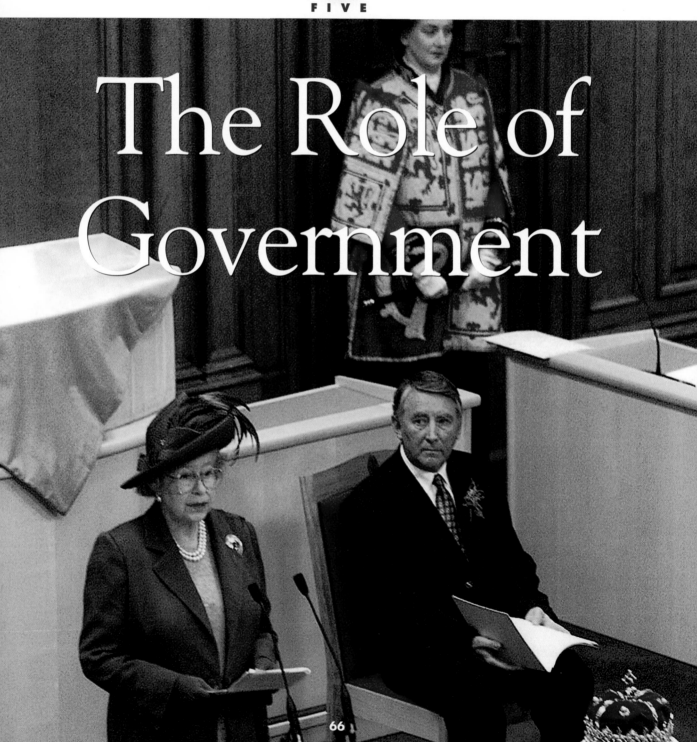

The Role of Government

"TODAY IS A HISTORIC DAY FOR SCOTLAND. IT IS A moment, rare in the life of any nation, when we step across the threshold of a new constitutional age. . . . I am pleased, therefore, to declare the Scottish Parliament open." As Queen Elizabeth spoke these words in Edinburgh, supersonic jets thundered overhead and bagpipers dressed in kilts broke into music. Hundreds of Scot flags fluttered in the wind. The occasion was the July 1999 inauguration of the new Scottish Parliament. In Edinburgh, 292 years earlier, the old Scottish Parliament voted itself out of existence and joined England in the historic Act of Union. Since then, Scotland had been ruled by the British Parliament, which met in London. Now Scotland would begin a fresh chapter in history with its own government.

But what does this mean? What will the new government be allowed to do, and what will it be restricted from doing?

Opposite: **Queen Elizabeth II opens the Scottish Parliament.**

A Look at the New Government

The Scottish Parliament cannot negotiate treaties with other countries. Nor can it control major taxes and money issues. When residents of Scotland travel, they will continue to use British—not Scottish—passports. Scotland's Parliament will preside over education, local government, local courts, social work, farming, and issues regarding the environment. As they have in the past, Scottish voters will send representatives to the British Parliament in London. The British Parliament will continue to control much of Scotland's destiny.

The British Parliament is divided into two houses—the House of Commons and the House of Lords. The Commons is made up of elected members who are called ministers of Parliament (M.P.s). The House of Commons is the true governing body of the United Kingdom. The Commons has 659 M.P.s, 72 of whom are from Scotland. The government is headed by the prime minister, a man or woman who is chosen by the majority political party. The new government formed in Scotland is based on the British system.

Members of the British Parliament convene in the House of Commons.

John A. Macdonald, Canadian Statesman

Many Scots became outstanding political leaders after they moved from Scotland to North America. John A. Macdonald (1815–1891) was born in Glasgow and sailed with his family to Canada when he was five years old. He entered politics and became the first prime minister of the Dominion of Canada. Many historians hail him as the father of the modern Canadian nation.

Scotland's Parliament has 129 members, each of whom represents a district in his or her home region. They are called M.S.P.s, or Members of the Scottish Parliament. The government is headed by an officer called the first minister, whose duties are similar to the prime minister's duties in London. The Scottish Parliament meets in Edinburgh, Scotland's capital. Members of Parliament are elected to four-year terms. However, as is true of the British Parliament, Scotland's M.S.P.s are free to vote "no confidence" in the government and call for new elections at any time.

Local governments and the judicial or court system also play important roles in Scottish government. Since 1996 the country's various towns and villages have been organized into thirty-two local authorities, These local authorities have responsibility over a variety of services including the administration of police and fire departments, and inspecting sanitation standards in restaurants and food markets. Many officers who serve on local authorities are unpaid and donate their time for the betterment of the community.

NATIONAL GOVERNMENT OF SCOTLAND

SCOTTISH GOVERNMENT (Edinburgh)

Executive Branch

(FIRST MINISTER)

Legislative Branch

(SCOTTISH PARLIAMENT (129 MEMBERS))

Judicial Branch

(COURT SYSTEM)

(LOCAL GOVERNMENTS)

BRITISH GOVERNMENT (London)

Executive Branch

(PRIME MINISTER)

(SECRETARY OF STATE FOR SCOTLAND)

Legislative Branch

(HOUSE OF COMMONS
(659 MINISTERS; 72 FROM SCOTLAND))

Judicial Branch

(HOUSE OF LORDS)

(BRITISH MONARCH)

Scotland has three levels of courts that deal with crimes. Serious crimes such as murder are heard by the High Court of Justice, which consists of a judge and a jury made up of fifteen citizens. Lower courts act on minor violations of the law. In the late 1990s approximately 5,700 people (a small number in comparison to most other countries) were being held in Scottish jails.

There is a downside to Devolution, or home rule. Many fear home rule will lead to complete independence for Scotland and Wales. Such a split would severely weaken the United Kingdom, one of the world's most stable democracies. However, it is impossible to predict the future on these matters.

Will the people of Scotland and Wales some day desire complete independence? Will such independence be politically harmful to the United Kingdom? Or will the Scots be satisfied with their present home-rule government? Only time will provide answers to these questions. In the meantime, Scotland will rely on London for major governmental decisions. A special officer, the secretary of state for Scotland, will remain Scotland's most powerful voice in the British government.

**Edinburgh,
Say it Right**

Edinburgh is spelled similar to Pittsburgh, but it is never pronounced like the name of that Pennsylvania city. Edinburgh is always pronounced *E-din-bor-o*.

A Look at the Capital

For centuries, Scotland's rulers lived at Edinburgh Castle. The castle stands on Castle Rock, an ancient volcano, which towers

A view of Edinburgh Castle

Edinburgh: Did You Know This?

Edinburgh has been the capital of Scotland since 1437. With about 448,850 residents, it is Scotland's second largest city.

Important landmarks: Edinburgh Castle, which sits on cliffs that rise above the city. The castle is connected to Holyrood Palace, the 16th-century royal Scottish residence, by a road known as the Royal Mile. The city is also home to many fine museums and art galleries, including the National Gallery of Scotland and the Royal Scottish Museum.

Altitude: 441 feet (134 m)

Average daily temperature: 38.6°F (3.7°C) in January and 58.3°F (10.5°C) in July

Average annual rainfall: 27 inches (69 cm)

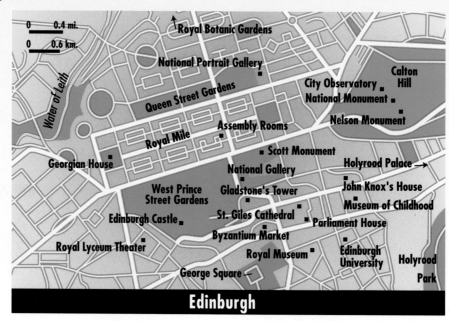

over the town. It is believed the Picts had a fortress on Castle Rock 2,500 years ago. Actually, the castle is a complex of buildings, all sacred to the Scottish soul. The oldest still standing part of the complex is Saint Margaret's Chapel, built around 1090. Edinburgh Castle, which was constructed in the 1400s, holds Scotland's crown jewels. Also on display is the Stone of Destiny.

Mons Meg Cannon

Edinburgh Castle was the scene of frightful battles and sieges. So many wars were fought there that, in the 1400s, James II of Scotland received an unusual wedding present—a massive cannon called Mons Meg. The cannon, which can be seen today at the castle, was the ultimate weapon of its time. It could shoot a 550-pound (249-kg) cannon ball to a distance of 2 miles (3.2 km).

Exit the castle and walk down Edinburgh's famous Royal Mile, a stretch of four twisting streets lined with shops and historic houses. One home belonged to John Knox, the fiery preacher who led the Scottish Reformation. On either side of

The Royal Mile

the Royal Mile are tiny alleyways called *closes*. The closes date back centuries, and each has a story to tell. Brodie's Close, for instance, contains the house of John Brodie, who was sentenced to be hanged in 1788. He tried—but failed—to cheat the hangman by wearing an iron collar under his high-necked sweater. A respected businessman by day and a thief at night, Brodie was the subject of Robert Louis Stevenson's famous story "The Strange Case of Dr. Jeckyll and Mr. Hyde."

Edinburgh is such a fascinating city that a tourist forgets it is Scotland's seat of government. Parliament Hall, which rises on the Royal Mile, is a reminder of the city's political importance. Built in the 1630s, it was here the old Scottish Parliament voted to join with England. The new Scottish Parliament building will be at the end of High Street, along the Royal Mile.

Scotland's Flag

Scotland's flag is based on Saint Andrews Cross and is called a *saltire*. Its X-shaped cross is white over a blue background. There are two stories connected to this symbol. The first deals with Saint Andrew, the patron saint of Scotland. Saint Andrew was sentenced to be crucified, but he asked Roman authorities to tie him to an X-shaped cross so his death would be unlike that of his leader, Jesus Christ. The second story dates to the year A.D. 832, when a Pict army saw a cross-shaped formation of clouds in the sky. The next day, inspired by the heavenly cross, the Picts won an important battle.

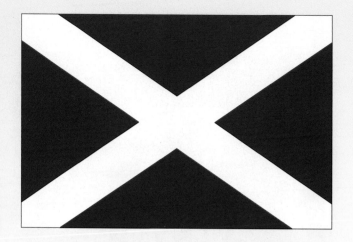

The Royal Mile ends at the Palace of Holyrood, where illustrious figures such as Mary, Queen of Scots and Bonnie Prince Charlie held court. One of Queen Mary's lovers was murdered at the palace, a killing which was probably ordered by the queen's jealous husband. It is said that King David I went hunting near here in the year 1128 and encountered a huge stag who lowered his horns and charged. Terrified, the king grabbed the stag's horns. Then, to his astonishment, the king discovered he was holding a crucifix, not the stag's menacing horns. In thanksgiving, King David built a church, and Holyrood has been a sacred spot ever since.

Because of frequent warfare, the old city was encircled by walls. It had nowhere to grow but up. Buildings were constructed five to eight stories high, and this in the days long before elevators. Crowding was so bad that writer Robert Louis Stevenson described conditions as "neighbor melting upon neighbor's shoulders." So, in the 1700s, when the threat of war diminished, Edinburgh's leaders decided to build a new city. Avenues were laid out in orderly gridlike patterns in contrast to the tangle of narrow streets in Old Edinburgh. Buildings went up in the magnificent neoclassical style that was popular at the time. Princes Street, today's shopping and entertainment thoroughfare, serves as the boundary between the New City and the Old City.

The Scottish National Anthem

To honor their nation, Scots sing the British national anthem, "God Save the Queen." Scotland has its own unofficial national anthem, "Flower of Scotland," which is often sung at soccer games. Its opening lines are:

O' Flower of Scotland when will we see your like again?
That fought and died for you wee bit of hill and glen,
And stood against him, proud Edward's Army.
And sent him homeward tae think again.

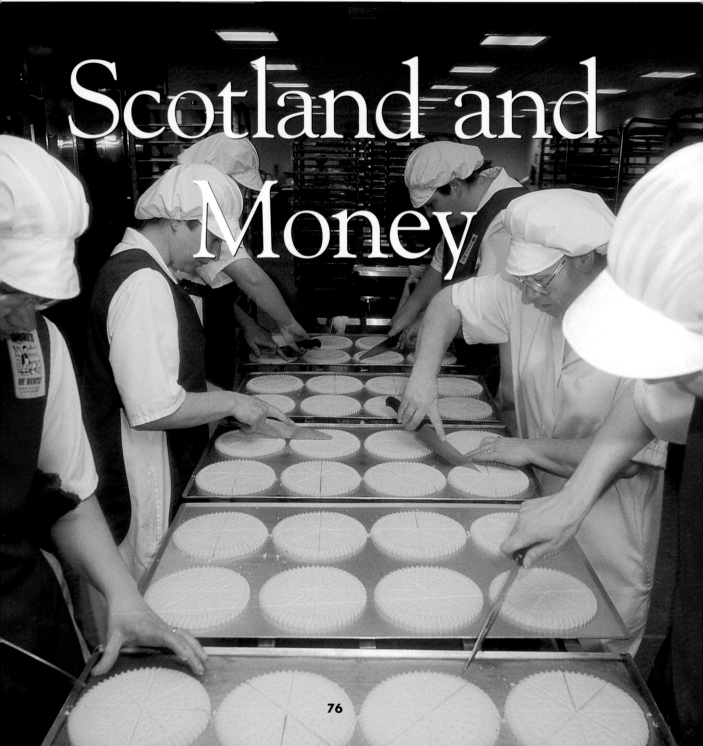

Scotland and Money

"CAST NOT A CLOUT TILL MAY BE OUT" IS AN OLD Scottish proverb meaning, "Don't get rid of your winter coat until the end of May." Dozens of jokes lampoon Scots as penny-pinchers. In truth, they work hard, play hard, and are not afraid to spend money. But they usually spend wisely and cannot be cheated out of a penny. The Scottish economy has had drastic ups and downs over the last fifty years. Yet Scot workers and business leaders have managed to pull the country through its financial challenges.

Opposite: **Slicing shortbread on a production line**

The Economy

Before World War II, Scotland's economy relied on shipbuilding, iron and steel production, and manufacturing. Today, heavy industry has a lesser role. More than two-thirds of Scottish adults are employed as service workers, meaning they perform services for customers instead of making a product. Baggers at a supermarket are service workers, as are teachers, doctors, and bank clerks. Tourists spend the equivalent of 3 billion U.S. dollars a year in Scotland, and the tourist industry employs 180,000 service people.

Workers

In the mid-1990s, the Scottish civilian workforce was made up of 1,155,000 men and 1,062,000 women.

The men earned an average of 335 pounds per week while women averaged only 244 pounds.

A woolen mill in the Lowlands   About one-fifth of Scottish workers are employed in manufacturing. Principal products include electrical machinery, woolens, and packaged food and beverages. Tweed goods and sweaters made in Scotland are still in demand throughout the world. The country is famous for its Scotch whiskey.

High-technology industries such as computers and Internet services are the fastest-growing and most exciting sector of the economy. More than 450 computer electronics firms operate in Scotland, and they employ 45,000 men and women. Scottish factories make more than one out of every three personal computers sold in Europe. Seven internationally known computer manufacturers have plants in Scotland. Edinburgh University is one of the world's top ten computer research centers.

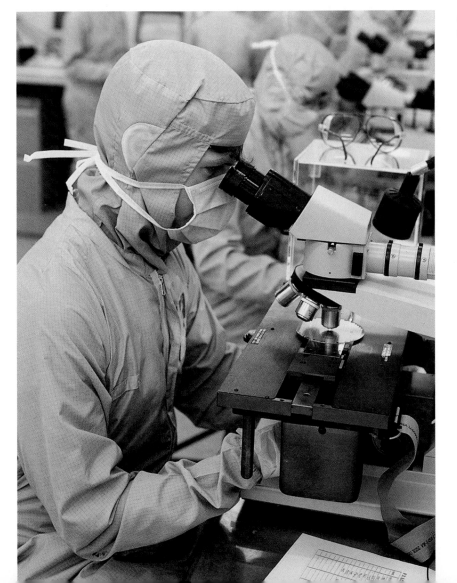

A technician at work in a computer company

Scotland's Silicon Glen

Silicon is a key ingredient in making computer chips, and the word *silicon* itself is synonymous with the computer revolution that is sweeping the earth. A stretch of highway between Glasgow and Edinburgh is called Silicon Glen. It is home to scores of multinational computer companies. The steel-and-glass building owned by Sun Microsystems looks as if it were magically transported from California's Silicon Valley. In the building, 600 technicians work producing computer components.

In 1973, the United Kingdom joined the European Union (EU). The EU is an organization of fifteen Western European nations that promotes trade and economic cooperation among its member states. As a market, the EU is huge. The fifteen nations have a combined population larger than that of the United States. Its total production of goods and services is greater than any single country in the world. As a member of the United Kingdom, Scotland's economy benefits from its inclusion in the EU. If Scotland becomes a separate nation, it will still be eligible for EU membership.

Some 270,000 Scots work in banks, insurance offices, and other business-related services. The Bank of Scotland, the country's oldest bank, was founded in 1695 and is still an active institution. Half of Europe's automatic teller machines are made in Scotland.

For centuries, coal was Scotland's most valued natural resource. By the end of the twentieth century, a new resource—offshore oil and gas—had replaced coal as a source of energy. Oil was first discovered under the choppy waters of the North Sea in the 1960s. Building oil-drilling platforms in this hostile section of the ocean took brilliant engineers and

courageous workers. Still, more than fifty such platforms went up. Submerged pipelines were laid to pump the crude oil to shipping facilities on the Orkney and Shetland Islands. The cities of Aberdeen and Peterhead became huge oil centers. Some 100,000 Scots hold oil-industry jobs, but a new resource is already emerging. Today, 45 percent of Scotland's electricity is produced by nuclear-powered generators.

This nuclear power station is located in Dumfries.

What Great Britain Grows, Makes, and Mines

Agriculture (1997)

Wheat	15,021,000 metric tons
Sugar beets	10,527,000 metric tons
Potatoes	7,125,000 metric tons

Manufacturing (1996; *value in British pounds*)

Electrical and optical equipment	18,270,000,000
Food and beverages	17,622,000,000
Paper, printing, and publishing	16,214,000,000

Mining (1996)

Crude petroleum	121,774,000 metric tons
Limestone	86,564,000 metric tons
Common sand and gravel	96,337,000 metric tons

About 60,000 people are employed in agriculture. More than half that number are small farmers who own their own land. Small farmers in the Highlands and the islands are called *crofters*. A typical crofter owns a house (a "croft"), a small patch of ground to grow vegetables and potatoes, and shares a larger field with other crofters where all graze their animals. Farmers are plagued by rocky and unfertile ground. Only one-fifth of Scottish soil is capable of growing crops in an efficient manner. Year after year, the country must rely on imports to feed its population. Much of Scottish agriculture is devoted to cattle and sheep ranching. More than 500,000 sheep graze the country's grasslands. The most productive soil is found in the Central Lowlands where farmers grow barley,

oats, wheat, potatoes, and rye. An enchanting folk song celebrates
the raising of rye:

> *If a body meet a body*
> *Comin' through the Rye,*
> *If a body kiss a body,*
> *Need a body cry?*

**Planting potatoes
on a farm in Angus**

Fishermen haul in a catch of salmon from the River Tweed.

ATLANTIC OCEAN

NORTH SEA

Lobster

Cod

Cod

Sheep

Sheep

Sheep

Salmon

Oats

Peterhead

Aberdeen

Dundee

E E E

Salmon

Cod

Glasgow

Edinburgh

C

Sheep

NORTHERN IRELAND

ENGLAND

O

O

O

Resources

Cereals	**C** Coal
Truck farms	**E** Water power
Dairy	**O** Oil
Livestock	
Pasture	

Fishing is another traditional Scottish resource undergoing change. The catch of herring, an old Scot staple, has diminished due to overfishing and the pollution of offshore waters. Fishing crews now probe the deep waters to pull in cod, haddock, and flounder. In the mid-1990s, the country had 2,800 fishing boats employing 5,400 people. Prime fishing ports are at Aberdeen and Peterhead.

An efficient transportation system is essential to keep a modern economy on the move. Scotland has more than 32,300 miles (52,000 km) of public roads. Despite this extensive road network, traffic jams can be ferocious. Almost 2 million vehicles are registered in Scotland, and they crowd the roads during rush hours. Train service

Adam Smith and the Invisible Hand

Under a capitalistic system, investors spend money to build factories and hope to grow rich in the process. This is a natural and correct procedure, according to Adam Smith (1723–1790), who is regarded as the founder of modern economics. Smith was born in Kirkcaldy, Scotland. In his book *The Wealth of Nations*, Smith argues that everyone benefits when people invest in factories and machinery. Such spending gives jobs to workers, who in turn spend money in food shops to the benefit of the shopkeeper. In this manner, the standard of living is raised, in Smith's words, "as if by an invisible hand."

between big cities is excellent, and all towns have a system of public buses. Many Scots live on islands and must rely on ferryboats to bring them to the mainland. Major airports operate at Glasgow, Edinburgh, Prestwick, and Aberdeen. The city of Aberdeen boasts the world's busiest helicopter landing facility. Helicopters race in and out of Aberdeen transporting crews to offshore oil drilling platforms.

Currency and Costs

The basic unit of Scottish currency is the pound sterling. The Scottish pound is tied directly to the British pound. Both currencies have equal value in stores throughout the United Kingdom. This means you can spend Scottish money in London or in Edinburgh without problems. Both currencies have the same exchange rate with foreign currencies. The rate of foreign exchange shifts up and down and sometimes may change dramatically in just a few months.

After a traveler masters Scot currency (and it's really quite simple), he or she will enter the stores to see what this money will buy. Be prepared for a shock.

Pounds and Pence

Scottish paper money comes in notes of £5, £10, £20, £50, and £100. There are 100 pence (p) per pound. Common coins are 1p, 5p, 10p, 20p, 50p, and £1. Now and then you'll see a £2 coin. The Scot £1 note has a picture of the Edinburgh Castle on one side. The £20 note honors the writer Sir Walter Scott by displaying his picture.

Hungry? Go to a McDonald's restaurant. You'll find these U.S. style fast food places in every major Scottish city. Order a Big Mac, fries, and a shake. In the year 2000, the charge for such a meal in Glasgow was £4, the equivalent of U.S.$6.40. That same McDonald's meal would cost U.S.$4 in Chicago. Scotland—and all of the United Kingdom—is an expensive place to visit or live.

Scots bemoan the sky-high prices they have to pay for consumer goods. Here are a few examples in U.S. dollars: A skirt at a Gap store that costs $30 in Los Angeles costs $55 in Aberdeen. A movie ticket is almost $14 in many Scottish theaters. Nike Air Jordan running shoes cost $125 in Scotland, while the same pair can be had for $80 in the United States. British trains charge the highest fares in all of Europe.

Why these high costs? Economists contend that high land prices lead to steep rents, so store owners are forced to charge more for goods. High taxes also enter into the picture. Consumers claim that greed on the part of store owners burdens them with one of the highest costs of living in the world. Inflated costs plague all residents of the United Kingdom, not just the Scots. Even Tony Blair, the British prime minister at the end of the twentieth century, has called his country "Ripoff Britain."

The Richest Man in the World

Andrew Carnegie (1835–1919) was born into poverty in Dunfermline. At age thirteen, Carnegie moved with his family to the United States, where they settled near Pittsburgh, Pennsylvania. Young Andrew worked shoveling coal into a blast furnace at a cotton factory. He earned $1.20 a week. Despite his meager paycheck, Carnegie saved money and made investments. He got a new job with the Pennsylvania Railroad and worked his way up from messenger boy to superintendent.

In 1864, Carnegie invested in iron and steel. He was ruthless in dealing with his business competitors and often stingy with his workers. By 1900, he was—by many estimates—the richest man in the world. He retired from business and proceeded to give away his money. Carnegie had little formal education but harbored a lifelong love of books. He endowed nearly 2,800 libraries in the United States and in Great Britain. He was also a major contributor to Tuskegee Institute, the mostly African-American college in Alabama. Why did he bestow these generous gifts? Carnegie told friends, "A man who dies rich, dies disgraced."

A Look at the Scots

A STORY—WHICH MIGHT BE MADE UP—TELLS OF AN English politician campaigning for office in Scotland. The politician said he was born an Englishman and he would die an Englishman, but he would still represent Scottish interests properly.

A Scottish heckler interrupted the politician. "Don't you ever want to become a Scotsman?" he asked.

"No," said the politician. "I repeat. I was born English and I shall die English."

The Scot said, "Man, have you no ambition?"

The story serves to remind us that Scots are British, they are not English, and they will always be a people apart.

Elements of the Population

In 1996, the estimated population of Scotland stood at 5,149,000. About 86 percent of Scottish people live in cities and towns, while 14 percent dwell in rural areas. Many rural areas have been suffering a population drain in recent years. Abandoned houses—even abandoned villages—are seen in the north and on the islands. In 1850, thirty-four of the Shetland Islands in the far north were occupied, whereas today only thirteen of the Shetlands are inhabited.

Opposite: **Kids cram into a phone booth in Edinburgh.**

They Are Scots, Not . . .

Scots are properly called Scots or Scottish people. They are not referred to as Scotch. After all, Scotch is a type of whiskey made in Scotland. However, if you make a mistake and call them Scotch, you will be forgiven. Just don't call them English.

An abandoned settlement on the Isle of Lewis

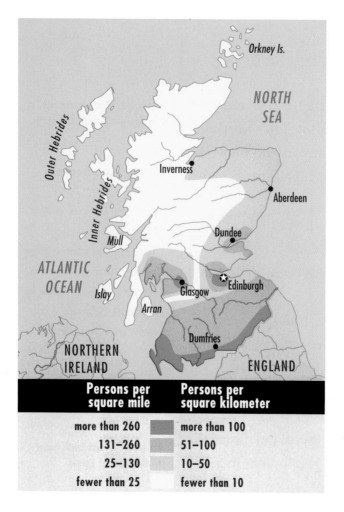

Persons per square mile		Persons per square kilometer
more than 260	▨	more than 100
131–260	▨	51–100
25–130	▨	10–50
fewer than 25	☐	fewer than 10

Population of Major Cities (1996 est.)

Edinburgh	448,850
Glasgow	616,430
Aberdeen	217,260
Dundee	150,250

The population density of Scotland is 169 people per square mile (65 per sq km), making Scotland an uncrowded country compared to most European nations. France, for example, has a population density of 279 people per square mile (108 per sq km). The uncrowded nature of rural Scotland can be seen on a train trip to the north, where sheep outnumber people and the train passes mile after mile of lonely mountains and forests. In many areas of the north, the population density drops to 10 people per square mile (4 per sq km).

Today, the Highlands contain only 373,000 residents. Many are old people living on pensions. The young dash off to find excitement and work in the big cities. One out of five jobs in the Highlands is in the tourist industry. U.S. and Canadian citizens of Scottish descent are frequent visitors as they try to feel the spirit of their ancestors who left this land for the New World.

Through the years, emigration has altered Scottish society. Most families in Scotland have had at least one member move to a foreign country seeking a new and bountiful life. This massive emigration has had a deep—and often negative—

Tartan, the Uniforms of the Clans

Highland clans once dressed in woolen kilts, scarves, and shirts woven in plaid patterns. Each clan wore its own distinguishing pattern. In Scotland, these patterns are called *tartans*. The tartans were so important to the fighting nature of the clans that in the 1700s the government prohibited men from wearing them in an attempt to pacify the Highlands. In modern times, foreign tourists with names like MacLeod or Mackay visit special shops in the Highlands to buy the tartan of their ancestors and display it in their homes.

effect on the people left behind. Scots complain that their best and brightest men and women have gone overseas. The United States and Canada, especially, have benefited from the Scot genius. Emigration has slowed in recent years, but its legacy continues to shape Scottish life.

About three out of every four Scots live in the Central Lowlands. This means three-fourths of Scotland's people live on one-sixth of its land. Edinburgh and Glasgow, both in the Central Lowlands, lie about 50 miles (80 km) apart. Both cities have extensive suburbs.

Who Lives in Scotland? (1992–1994; for entire United Kingdom)	
White	93.7%
Asian Indian	1.8%
Pakistani	1.4%
Black	1.4%
Other and not stated	1.6%

Who Are the Scots?

The vast majority of Scots are descendants of the Picts, the Scots, and the Norse peoples who came in ancient times. If

What's in a Name?

Over the last 150 years, the most popular names given to Scot babies were Andrew for boys and Emma for girls.

there is a "Scot look" it can be seen in young people with fair skin and blue eyes. Red and blond hair are common in children. World travelers hail the beauty of Scottish people, especially the women.

Any resident of the United Kingdom who lives permanently in Scotland is considered a Scottish citizen. Thus Scots include thousands of people of English, Welsh, and Irish heritage. In the 1950s and 1960s, a wave of immigrants from India, Pakistan, the West Indies, Africa, and other parts of the former British Empire reached the United Kingdom. Many of them moved to Scotland, where they now make up 1.3 percent of the population.

Scots speak the English language—well, sort of. Americans and many English claim they have difficulty understanding Scottish brogue, or pronunciation, especially when it is spoken by an older person. But be patient and accept the Scottish accent as a colorful use of English. Remember that *sang* means "song," and *tae* means "to"; *aye* means "yes," *tak* means "take," and *Ye comin tae the jiggin?* is translated as "Are you going to the dance?" Scottish brogue is musical and lends itself to poetry. And don't forget, Scots have trouble understanding Americans—ya know.

Gaelic is an ancient language, but it is far from being dead in Scotland. An estimated 80,000 people use Gaelic in everyday

A Few Gaelic Words

The word *Gaelic* is pronounced with a soft *a* sound, like "garlic" without the *r*. The language was first brought to Scotland by Celtic people from Ireland. Over the centuries, Scottish Gaelic evolved and became a quite different language from Irish Gaelic. Here are some examples of Scottish Gaelic words:

Hello.	*Hallo.*
Come in.	*Thig a-staigh.*
Thank you.	*Tapadh leat.*
Today	*An-diugh*
Yesterday	*An-dé*
Goodbye.	*Mar sin leat.*

speech. However, no one in Scotland speaks only Gaelic and is unable to use English. The Gaelic language faded in importance many years ago, when the government launched an English-only movement in Scotland. Gaelic is now enjoying a revival with the fervor of Scottish independence. Many train stations in Scotland list the English name of a town in red and the Gaelic name in green. Spoken Gaelic is concentrated in the Highlands and on the Hebrides Islands. It is estimated that 60 percent of the people living on the Isle of Skye use Gaelic regularly.

A Gaelic/English sign

A People of Genius

In 1928, a Scottish researcher named Alexander Fleming (1881–1955) closed up his laboratory and went on vacation. Carelessly, he left a lab dish filled with germs uncovered, and a tiny piece of mold called *penicillium notatum* fell into the open dish. When he returned from his vacation, Fleming saw that the mold had killed most of the germs. He had discovered penicillin, a medicine that would save more lives than were lost in all the world wars of the twentieth century combined. Fleming was awarded the Nobel Prize for Medicine for his incredible contribution to world health.

Alexander Fleming

A Look at the Scots **93**

In 1997, a team of scientists at Edinburgh's Roslin Institute created a sheep by the process of cloning. The scientists called the sheep Dolly. It was the first large animal produced through cloning. To make a clone, scientists manipulate a small genetic sampling of the original subject. Many people are troubled by cloning because they believe the procedure imitates the work of God.

Through the ages, Scots have shown a genius for invention that is astonishing for such a tiny country with a small population. The telephone was invented in the United States

Dolly, the cloned sheep

Alexander Graham Bell and his telephone invention, circa 1876

by Alexander Graham Bell (1847–1922), a Scotsman born in Edinburgh. The first bicycle with foot pedals was built in 1839 by a Scottish blacksmith Kirkpatrick Macmillan. The pneumatic (air-filled) tire was devised by John Dunlop (1840–1921), a Scottish veterinarian who wanted to make his son's tricycle run more smoothly. Logarithms are mathematical tables drawn up by the Scotsman John Napier (1550–1617). In the days before computers, logarithms allowed engineers to multiply and divide large numbers in a relatively easy manner. James Simpson (1811–1870) was a Scottish doctor who pioneered the use of chloroform to ease the pain of surgery.

The list goes on and on. It is truly amazing how people around the world have benefited from inventions fashioned in tiny Scotland.

A People
of Faith

WITH ABOUT 2 MILLION DECLARED MEMBERS, THE Church of Scotland is the country's largest church. It is a Presbyterian faith, governed by a team of about 1,250 officers called elders, who are elected by church members. The Church of Scotland is often called the Kirk, an old Celtic word.

Until recent years, the Church of Scotland dominated life in the country. In many ways it was a repressive church, quick to condemn sin and reluctant to forgive it. Especially important were laws observing the Sabbath. Scottish towns were deathly quiet on Sundays. Shops were closed. Children

"Doctor Livingstone, I Presume?"

In the nineteenth century, Presbyterian churches sent missionary teams to remote parts of the world to spread the word of Christ. David Livingstone (1813–1873) was a Scottish missionary doctor who plunged into the unknown interior of Africa to preach and to treat suffering people. He also explored wild regions of the continent, sighting the marvelous Victoria Falls in 1855. Livingstone was so isolated in Africa that people feared he had died. In 1869, the *New York Herald* sent journalist Henry Stanley to find the doctor. After a two-year quest, the exhausted and half-starved Stanley discovered the Scot physician in a tiny African settlement. Stanley offered the famous greeting, "Doctor Livingstone, I presume?"

Religions in Scotland:

Church of Scotland:	746,000
Roman Catholic:	350,000
Other churches:	over 100,000

were forbidden to play outdoors. Even reading the Sunday newspapers was considered a sinful activity. Restrictive laws regarding the Sabbath did not ease until the 1950s.

Today, church attendance is in decline. A census taken in 1995 counted 575,000 adults and 171,000 children as regularly attending members of the Church of Scotland.

Pews inside Scottish churches are sparsely filled.

The King James Bible

King James VI of Scotland achieved fame in 1603 when he became king of both England and Scotland. The king was a deeply religious man who wanted to make the miracles of the Bible more accessible to his subjects. In 1604, James appointed a committee of fifty scholars to translate the Bible into English. At the time, most Bibles were written in Latin, a language known only to the priests, the educated, and the rich.

The King James Version of the Bible first appeared in 1611. The book was written in the form of English in common usage. Despite the fact it was written by a committee, its passages contained energy, drama, and poetry. Most important, the King James Version spoke directly to the people. A peasant farmer who managed to learn to read could study the Bible first hand, free from the interpretations of priests. The King James Version of the Bible became the best-selling book ever printed.

These figures represent a sharp decrease from just ten years earlier. The church remains a strong institution only in the areas where Gaelic is still spoken. Some Scots are saddened by the demise of the Kirk because they believe it brought order and stability to their communities.

Many Faiths

Freedom of religion is guaranteed by law in Scotland. Scots are Catholics, Baptists, Methodists, Episcopalians, Jews, or members of Presbyterian branches other than the Church of Scotland. Recent arrivals to the country brought their old religions with them. Islam, Buddhism, Hinduism, and Sikhism are all practiced in Scotland.

Roman Catholicism is Scotland's second largest religion. Many Catholics are of Irish heritage. Irish have moved to Scotland in large numbers beginning with the Irish Potato Famine in the 1840s. Irish migration picked up again during the two world wars, when Scotland desperately needed factory

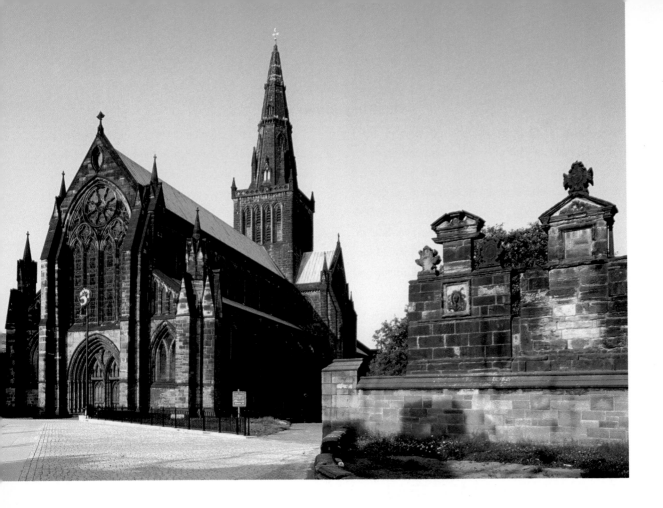

The Cathedral Church of St. Mungo, Glasgow

hands. Irish Roman-Catholic communities are scattered around Scotland. Catholics are the majority in the industrial town of Coatbridge, for instance, and Glasgow's East End section is Irish and heavily Catholic.

For the most part, the Irish Catholics and the Scottish Presbyterians get along quite well. Irish and Scots, after all, are distant cousins. Many Scots are descended from the Picts who came from Ireland centuries ago. On Sundays, people of Scottish heritage attend their Kirk while Irish Catholics go to mass. Often, the two church buildings stand just a block from each other.

Important Religious Holidays

Good Friday (moveable)	(March–April)
Easter (moveable)	(March–April)
Christmas	December 25

But the peace is shattered during soccer season. A holy war breaks out when the Glasgow Rangers (favored by the city's Scots) play the Glasgow Celtics (the darlings of the Irish). This traditional game is called the "Old Firm." At Old Firm contests, players and fans taunt each other. Fights break out on the field and in the stands. Most people agree that religious rivalry is the root cause of this soccer game's passions. Centuries ago, Catholics and Protestants fought bloody religious battles on Scottish soil.

Scotland's Patron Saint

A legend says a holy man named Regulus lived on the Greek Island of Patras, where he was entrusted to watch over the grave of Saint Andrew. In a dream, Regulus was told to dig up the bones of Saint Andrew and carry them by ship to the west. There, he should rebury the bones and establish a church and a city on the site of the new grave. Regulus did as he was instructed. He was shipwrecked and almost drowned off the coast of Scotland. But Regulus managed to drag the bones ashore, where he founded the town of Saint Andrews. Soon thereafter Saint Andrew became the patron saint of Scotland.

Scots at Ease

TOUR SCOTLAND AND YOU WILL SEE FARMERS AT WORK IN the fields and business people dashing madly along city streets. You may wonder if these people ever pause to rest. But away from their jobs, Scots enjoy music, the arts, good food, sports, and parties. Above all, this is a country of readers, and it has generated some of the best writers in the English-speaking world.

Literature

One Sunday morning long ago, Robert Burns sat in church. Sitting stiffly ahead of him was a dignified and very proper lady. She wore an exquisite bonnet and a blouse with a high collar. Suddenly, Burns spotted a head louse, a tiny bug that nests in dirty hair. The bug raced about the lady's neck and scalp unnoticed by her. The scene inspired Burns to write a poem called "To a Louse."

> *Ye ugly, creepin, blastit wonner,*
> *Detested, shunn'd by saunt an' sinner,*
> *How daur ye set your fit upon her -*
> *Sae fine a lady!*
> *Gae somewhere else and seek your dinner*
> *On some poor body.*

This is Robert Burns—shocking, earthy, willing to write about mice, lice, or anything that struck his fancy. Burns was born in 1759 in the small village of Alloway. His father was a farmer. Despite his success as a poet, Burns worked as a farmer

Happy New Year!

Every New Year's Eve, people the world over join in a familiar song. Few realize the song was written by Robert Burns. "Auld Lang Syne" are words in the Scottish dialect that mean "Old Long Since," or "Days Gone By." Burns claimed he once heard an elderly man singing this refrain. The melody comes from an old Scottish ballad.

A depiction of the betrothal of Burns and Highland Mary

most of his life. He never lost the rough humor and folksy wisdom of the dirt-scratching peasant. When not farming, he wrote powerful poetry. He also loved music and gave new words to centuries-old country songs. In this way he created folk song masterpieces such as "Comin thro' the Rye" and "Green Grow the Rashes, O." Burns married his childhood sweetheart, and they had nine children. He died in 1796 when he was only thirty-seven. He is Scotland's national poet, and he is beloved in the country today.

Burns could and did write in the finest English used in London. However, some of his most sparkling poems and songs were rendered in the Scottish dialect, the colorful language of his plowman neighbors. Most books of Burns's poetry have a glossary in the back that serves as a dictionary of the Scottish dialect. Aided by this glossary, it is relatively easy to follow Burns' words. For example, from the "To a Louse" poem: *How daur ye set your fit upon her/ Sae fine a lady!* In this line *daur* is "dare," *fit* is "feet," and *sae* is "so." Now you can imagine Burns' comic indignation when he silently demands of this creepy-crawler, "How dare you set your feet on so fine a lady!" Reading Burns in the Scottish dialect requires a little work, but the rewards are worth the effort.

Sir Walter Scott (1771–1832) was born in Edinburgh. A childhood disease (probably polio) left him crippled, but he still took long walks in the fields outside of the city. During the walks he dreamed up the plots and characters for his novels, most of them historical fiction. His books *Ivanhoe* and *The Talisman* were widely read. He immersed readers in the lives of kings and queens as well as village shopkeepers. Scott enjoyed success during his lifetime, but his popularity declined in the 1900s. Today, he is a writer every educated person knows of, but few have read one of his books from cover to cover. This is a pity because Scott is a masterful storyteller with much to say to modern readers.

Sir Walter Scott

Robert Louis Stevenson

A quest for adventure and a hunger for travel dominated the life of Robert Louis Stevenson (1850–1894). Born in Edinburgh to a wealthy family, Stevenson suffered a lung disease as a child and remained sickly most of his life. Seeking an agreeable climate, he traveled to Europe, the United States, and the exotic South Sea Islands. The romance of faraway places inspired him to write exciting novels such as *Kidnapped* and *Treasure Island.* His prose had the rare power to

capture the attention of young readers as well as adults. He earned a comfortable income from the sale of his books. Stevenson bought a farm on the South Seas island of Samoa and settled in as a gentleman planter. He died there at age forty-four, ending the life of an adventurer. At his instruction, his gravestone carries the lines of one of his poems:

Here he lies where he longed to be;
Home is the sailor, home from the sea,
And the hunter home from the hill.

Harry Potter author
J.K. Rowling

Modern Scottish writers have loyal followers in Scotland and around the world. Irvine Welsh's 1993 novel *Trainspotting* told of the grim lives of Glasgow drug addicts; the novel was made into a popular movie. James Kelman's 1994 novel *How Late It Was, How Late* won several literary awards. Alasdair Gray writes fantasies that he illustrates with his own drawings. The poet Jakie Kay presents the experience of being a black citizen of Scotland.

Without question, Scotland's most successful contemporary writer is Edinburgh resident J. (for Joanne) K. Rowling. Rowling combines magic, humor, and scary stuff to create the best-selling series of children's books in modern times. Her first book, *Harry Potter and the Sorcerer's Stone*, appeared in 1997, and it was followed by *Harry Potter and the Chamber of Secrets*. They tell of an orphan boy who discovers on his eleventh birthday that he is really a wizard who can perform magic. Abracadabra! Off he goes on fantastic adventures at wizard schools and castles. Rowling's first two books sold 2 million copies in Great Britain and 5 million copies in the United States, and they were translated into twenty-eight languages. This wild popularity came about largely because kids told other kids how exciting the stories were. One children's book editor said of Rowling's phenomenal success, "It happened on the playground."

A Few National Treasures

Scotland has more than 400 museums supported by the government. The National Museum of Scotland in Edinburgh tells the story of Scotland from prehistoric times to the Industrial Revolution and beyond. Featured at the National Museum is a double-action steam engine built by James Watt in 1786, a device that might be called the machine that changed the world. Also in Edinburgh is the National Gallery of Scotland, which holds paintings by European masters including Diego Rodríguez de Silva Velásquez and Paul

The Boy Who Wouldn't Grow Up

One of the most enduring tales to come out of Scotland is the play *Peter Pan*, by James Barrie (1860–1937). Born in the town of Kirriemuir, Barrie wrote many successful novels and plays, but none had the long-lasting fame of the adventures of Peter Pan and the fairy Tinkerbell. The always playful Peter was dubbed "The Boy Who Wouldn't Grow Up."

Screen Stars

Scotland has spawned movie actors that have achieved fame in Hollywood. David Niven (1909–1983) and Deborah Kerr (b. 1921) were born in Scotland and became Hollywood idols in the 1940s and 1950s. Today's star Sean Connery was born in Edinburgh in 1930 and became a superstar as the spy James Bond.

The Museum of Childhood

Along High Street on Edinburgh's Royal Mile is the Museum of Childhood. It contains a marvelous collection of old model trains, dolls, teddy bears, and toys. The museum was founded in 1955 by a local politician who claimed he hated children. "I eat [children] for breakfast," the founder once grumbled. Today, excited kids are its primary guests, and it is called "the noisiest museum in the world."

Cézanne. The Glasgow Art Gallery and Museum contains paintings as well as a fascinating collection of ancient arms and armor. Glasgow's Hunterian Art Gallery displays paintings by James Whistler, an American-born artist who spent much of his life in Europe.

An imaginative hedgerow sculpture at Pitmedden Gardens

Scottish gardens are world famous. The Crarae Gardens, which overlook Loch Fyne, are nestled in a woodland and explode with rhododendrons in the spring. The Pitmedden Gardens near Aberdeen date back to the 1600s and feature box hedges laid out in intricate patterns. Also at Pitmedden is the Museum of Farming

Life. Set under a steel and glass dome, the Botanic Gardens in Glasgow contain a delightful collection of orchids. Some 17,000 types of plants are found in Edinburgh's Royal Botanic Garden. The Royal Botanic Garden also serves as a research center for botanists.

Scattered over Scotland are dozens of historic houses that have been maintained and restored to display their original splendor. Hopetoun House near Edinburgh is one of Scotland's finest stately homes. The original Hopetoun House was constructed in 1707, and many wings have been added according to an elegant horseshoe-shaped plan. Sir Walter Scott's house near Melrose was finished in 1824 and serves as a shrine to the great writer. Scott called the house Abbotsford, and inside is the sword once owned by the Highland warrior Rob Roy. Visitors to Abbotsford can also see Scott's collection of 9,000 rare books and the tiny study where the writer worked.

Scotland's most dramatic national treasures are its castles. Over the ages, they functioned as fortresses whose thick walls withstood invading armies. They were also glittering homes for kings and queens, and some were courts of law complete with dungeons and terrible instruments of torture. Today, the

The Green Ghost

What's an old house or a castle without a ghost? One of Scotland's most famous ghosts is the Green Lady who haunts Crathes Castle near Aberdeen. This spirit, dressed in green, is sometimes seen holding a baby in her arms. She was last sighted in the 1980s.

The Lighthouse Builder

Robert Stevenson (1772–1850) was an engineer who designed magnificent lighthouses. The twenty-three lighthouses he built along the coast of the United Kingdom are glorious unions of engineering and art. His grandson, the writer Robert Louis Stevenson, called them "tall memorials to catch the dying sun." The elder Stevenson's Bell Rock Lighthouse, near Dundee, has inspired paintings and poetry. Over the years, four generations of the family built ninety-seven lighthouses that dot the Scottish coast today.

Scotland's Castles

Some of Scotland's castles are in marvelous conditions. Others are roofless ruins. Each has a unique history. Here are just a few of Scotland's castles that are worth a visit:

Balmoral Castle, near Aberdeen, is the official Scottish residence of the British royal family. The Queen of England and her family delight in spending the summer months there.

The grounds of Brodie Castle at Forres have been owned by the Brodie family since 1160, and members of the Brodie family still live in one wing.

History abounds at Dunnottar Castle (pictured above), near Aberdeen, where William Wallace fought a battle in 1297 and Mary, Queen of Scots visited in 1562.

Stirling Castle, outside of the town of Stirling, stands on a rocky crag that was a military fortress even during the Iron Age. A row of cannons along its parapet attests that battles continued here until the 1600s.

Cawdor Castle, near Nairn, is tied to a legend. It is said that a prince was told in a dream to walk with his donkey and build a castle on the spot where the donkey paused to rest. The donkey stopped under a broad tree, and Cawdor Castle was built there in the 1300s. This castle was the setting for Shakespeare's tragedy *Macbeth*.

castles are showplaces of ancient architecture. Almost all of Scotland's castles are open to the public. Some people spend an entire vacation looking over these ancient structures and trying to discern what stories they have to tell.

Music and Dance

Think of Scottish music and you can almost hear the sound of bagpipes. A bagpipe is played by blowing air into a leather bag and then forcing the air through five wooden pipes to create a melody. It is believed the ancient Romans used a form of bagpipe and introduced it to Scotland centuries ago. Bagpipes provide somber music for funerals as well as bouncy tunes for folk dancing. Slow, haunting melodies called the *pibroch* are rendered by a solo bagpipe player. With good reason, the bagpipe is thought of as Scotland's national instrument.

Scottish rock groups such as the Silly Wizards and the Battlefield Band blend ancient Celtic music with rock and pop rhythms. Traditional Scottish folk music is played in the clubs of Glasgow. A Glasgow folk group called the Incredible String Band has won international acclaim. Jean Redpath is a Scottish vocalist well known for her renditions of Robert Burns songs and other traditional Scottish music. Ancient Celtic music lives through *ceilidh* bands. Ceilidh (a Gaelic word for "visit") is lively music played by a band that includes flutes, accordions, and whistles. Classical music lovers flock to the Royal Scottish National Orchestra, the Scottish Chamber Orchestra, and the Scottish Opera. Aberdeen hosts the International Youth Festival of Music and the Arts, which showcases jazz groups, chamber groups, and choirs whose performers are under twenty-five years of age.

Music rocks the capital city during the Edinburgh International Festival held every August. The festival lasts two weeks, and in that time the city's population doubles as

Forbidden Pipes

After the Battle of Culloden in 1746, the government banned the playing of bagpipes in an attempt to bring peace to the Highlands. In the past, Highlanders marched to battle behind a piper. The ban did not work, as Highlanders played their beloved pipes in secret.

visitors from all over the world squeeze in. It is a combination art fair, film fair, and book fair. But music explodes everywhere—rock, classical, folk, jazz, and opera. Of course, bagpipes prevail. The highlight of the fair is the Military Tattoo, a marching band of pipers and drummers. More than 200,000 guests attend performances of this precision marching group during the festival. The Military Tattoo's rallying song is every Scot's favorite "Scotland the Brave."

The Military Tattoo assembled at the Edinburgh International Festival

Scotland (blue) and the U.S. (white) compete in a World Cup qualifying soccer game.

Sports

Scotland's favorite sport is soccer, or football, as Scots and most people around the world call the game. Football is played on every level—in high schools and universities, and by city kids in empty lots. Professional football draws the most fans. Millions of people attend professional matches during the season, which extends from October to May. The Scottish Cup is the championship prize coveted by pro teams. Every four years, a Scottish national team is assembled to compete for the European Cup. The biggest treasure of all is the World Cup, the grand event that draws teams from around the earth. During important international contests, the streets of Scotland's cities become strangely hushed. Everyone is inside glued to their television sets, following every flight of the ball.

The game of golf was invented in Scotland. The first written mention of golf came in 1457, when the Scottish king

St. Andrews Golf Club

James II banned the game because his soldiers spent too much time on the golf course when they should be marching or practicing archery. Some critics claim Scots still spend too much time playing golf. There are more than 400 golf courses in Scotland. The most honored is the private Royal and Ancient Golf Club at Saint Andrews. If you want to play at one of Saint Andrews other courses, you have to book months or even years in advance. In 1999, Paul Lawrie of Aberdeen became a national hero when he won the British Open, becoming the first Scot to win the prestigious match in sixty-nine years.

Scots are avid tennis players. Rugby, a gift from England, is a popular team sport. Outdoor basketball courts are found in all the big towns. The game of curling probably began in Scotland some 300 years ago. Curling is a winter sport in which teams try to slide a stone over ice onto a prescribed circle. One team member does the sliding while others assist the passage

Scotland's curling team participating in the World Championships

of the stone by sweeping the ice with brooms. Scots also ski and ice-skate during the winter months. Hiking or hill walking is the favorite family sport. In September, a special Ben Nevis Race is held, where amateur mountain climbers trek up Scotland's highest peak.

Tossing the caber at the Highland Games

Astonishing sports prevail during the annual Highland Games. Though called Highland Games, they actually are played at more than 100 different locations in Scotland. The cities of Cowal, Oban, and Braemar are their most important sites. The games are billed as track meets, but they are much more. They began centuries ago, possibly when clan chiefs wanted to find the strongest and swiftest men for their armies. A feature of the Braemar games is throwing the *caber*, a tree trunk about 20 feet (6 m) long and weighing some 145 pounds (66 kg). Lifting and balancing the caber is in itself a feat. Throwing the caber a good distance is a remarkable achievement. The Highland Games also feature bagpipe music, folk songs, and dance.

Everyday Life

READ ITS POETRY AND LISTEN TO ITS SONGS, AND YOU know that Scotland is a romantic country. But everyday life consists of work, play, and going to school. These are not romantic pursuits, yet Scots still have fun in the workaday world.

Opposite: **A country woman spinning wool**

Scotland Around the Clock

It is seven in the morning, and Scots leave home to report to their jobs. Farmers have already been up and about for hours, but these days less than 2 percent of Scots work on farms. City people and suburbanites begin their day with a breakfast that includes tea with milk and sugar and oatmeal or dry cereal. Morning traffic jams are frustrating, but most people take

The Queen Street station in Glasgow

trains or buses to work. Many buses are double-deckers and give passengers sitting on the upper level an interesting view of the neighborhoods. Only one Scottish city, Glasgow, has a subway. At nine in the morning, children dash off to school. They walk or take public trains or buses. There are few special school buses operating in Scotland.

The Famous Scottish Kilt

For everyday purposes, Scots dress the same as people in the United States or in the rest of Europe. But for special celebrations, Scots don the knee-length skirt called the kilt. The kilt probably originated in the Highlands. It has a tartan (plaid) design signifying one of the Highland clans. Women may wear kilts, but traditionally the skirts are men's attire. A very personal but nagging question persists: What does a Scotsman wear under his kilt? A true Scotsman will never tell. What he wears (or doesn't wear) under his kilt is a national secret.

Enjoying a quick lunch at a chip shop

Scots live in apartment houses, row houses, and huge complexes called council houses. Detached houses, separated on all sides from neighboring houses, are the exception in built-up areas. A 1995 survey said 58 percent of Scottish families owned their own homes while the others rented. Home ownership has grown rapidly in recent years, and 80 percent of renters claim they would like to own a house but cannot afford the purchase price.

Lunch comes at noon for working people. Those in a hurry eat at fast food places such as the U.S. imports McDonald's and KFC. Traditional Scottish fast food is served at the chip shop, or "chipper," where customers consume fried potatoes and deep fried fish. In either case, greasy fried food is all too often gobbled up by Scots. As a result, Scotland has one of the highest heart-attack rates in the world. Slowly, as Scots learn that food laden with fats and oils is fatal to their health, more and more vegetarian restaurants and health food shops are opening.

When health problems arise, a Scot does not have to pay for a doctor or a hospital visit. All citizens of the United Kingdom are part of the National Health Service (NHS), a tax-supported institution that provides doctor and hospital care. The NHS began in 1948, and at first the people were pleased with their health care. Today, the system is the subject of bitter complaints. The problem is money. The United Kingdom spends only 6.8 percent of its national income on health care, whereas the United States spends 13.5 percent on health services. France, which also has a national health-care system, has 362 patients for each doctor, while the United Kingdom averages 1,885 patients per doctor. Dissatisfaction with the NHS is the subject of everyday chatter in Scotland and the rest of the United Kingdom. Many people no longer trust their health-care network.

The main meal for most city and suburban dwellers comes at home in the evening. Scottish food is simple, with perhaps too much emphasis on meat. Roast lamb, roast beef, and steaks from Aberdeen-Angus cattle are favorites. All meals are served with potatoes and bread. If a family wants take-outs, someone will dash over to the nearest "curry shop." Small restaurants owned by immigrants from India and Pakistan have sprung up everywhere since the 1960s, and Scots love the spicy curry dishes.

Haggis

The Scottish national dish is a concoction called *haggis*. It is made by chopping up the heart, liver, and lungs of a sheep, putting these ingredients in a bag made of the sheep's stomach, and boiling the bag and its contents. Does this sound icky? Yes! Is it unhealthy? Certainly, because haggis has a very high fat content. Today, Scots eat the dish only on certain holidays. Tourists try haggis to experience Scotland of old. Surprisingly, haggis does not taste as bad as the ingredients would make it seem.

After dinner, Scots read, watch TV, or go to the movies. When homework is completed, the kids may be allowed to run out to a noisy video game parlor. Adults visit the local pub. Pubs (short for public houses) are taverns that serve beer and liquor. Suburban and small-town pubs tend to be family oriented. Children are allowed into the pubs with their parents, but they are served only soft drinks.

The workaday routine is broken by holidays. New Year's Eve (called *Hogmanay*) is a more important holiday than Christmas. A tradition is to go "first footing" to visit neighbors and be the first foot to step inside the door in the new year. Christmas celebrations are similar to those in the United States, with gift-giving and decorating a tree. Christmas was not an official holiday in Scotland until 1967. Burns Night, on

January 25, honors the beloved poet with family readings of his works. On Halloween, children dress in costumes and knock on neighbors' doors. But instead of simply chanting "trick or treat" the kids are expected to sing a song or act out a play before they receive their candy.

National Holidays in Scotland:

New Year's Day	January 1
Good Friday	moveable (March–April)
First Monday in May	(bank holiday)
Last Monday in May	(bank holiday)
First Monday in August	(bank holiday)
Christmas	December 25
Boxing Day	December 26

Education

By law, all Scottish children from the ages of five to sixteen must attend school. Children under twelve go to primary schools, while those twelve to sixteen attend classes at secondary schools. Just about all schools require students to wear uniforms. The uniform includes a school badge and a distinctive school necktie.

Students in a secondary school science class

The School Tragedy That Shook Scotland

Normally, rural Scotland enjoys a peaceful, crime-free way of life. Some farm families don't even lock their doors at night. But, sadly, no community is safe from a madman with a gun. In the tiny town of Dunblane, a forty-three-year-old loner who was known locally as "Mr. Creepy" charged into a primary school. Once inside, he drew a pistol and killed sixteen kids and a teacher. The senseless shootings took place in March 1996. Scots were horrified and dumbfounded. Such nightmares simply did not happen in their schools. Said the school's headmaster, "Evil visited us yesterday, and we don't know why."

A view of one of the colleges at St. Andrews University

Students attend classes from nine in the morning until four in the afternoon. Reading, writing, and mathematics are stressed in primary schools. Secondary pupils study history, language (usually French), and computer sciences. The average class size is nineteen pupils per teacher in primary schools, and twelve pupils per teacher in secondary schools. Summer vacation lasts six weeks. The school system is excellent. Scots point with pride to the fact that their students regularly outperform English children in standardized math and reading tests.

After completing secondary school, qualified young people may pursue higher education. Scotland has thirteen universities with about 54,000 full-time and 190,000 part-time students. Edinburgh and Glasgow are the country's largest universities. Saint Andrews University, founded in 1412, is the third-oldest in Great Britain. Scotland also has nine institutions of higher education in which students study music, tourism, nursing, drama, or agriculture.

A Tour of Glasgow

Glasgow is Scotland's largest city and it contains all the elements typical of urban life. In the city live the rich, the poor, and the homeless. Many Scots consider it a city on the rise, while others denounce it as a place of shattered dreams.

In 1900, Glasgow had a population of more than 1 million and was Great Britain's second largest city, behind London. Its shipyards hummed with activity. Fabulous luxury liners such as the *Queen Elizabeth* and the *Queen Mary* were built on Glasgow's river, the Clyde. The city's working-class neighborhoods had a grimy look, but they held stable families. Nearby towns such as Motherwell, Clydebank, Greenock, Paisley, Hamilton, and Coatbridge became the city's industrial suburbs. Then, a few years after World War II, the shipyards slowed their production and factories started closing down. Today the population of Glasgow is around 600,000 and falling. Crime, alcoholism, and drug addiction are nagging problems.

Despite its faults, tourists and residents find excitement in Glasgow. It is home to the Scottish Opera and the Scottish National Symphony. The Glasgow Citizens Theater is perhaps Scotland's best. Nightlife and the movie scene are lively. Glasgow has seventy public parks. Well-to-do residents and tourists go to the West End to enjoy its glitzy shops and restaurants.

The Glasgow Boys

In the late 1800s, Glasgow was the scene of an exciting art movement. Painters such as James Guthrie and Robert McGregor lived and worked in the city. They painted peasant life and scenes at marketplaces. At the time, Edinburgh was considered Scotland's capital of art and culture, and "snooty" Edinburgh critics gave little recognition to Glasgow painters. European art-lovers, however, were thrilled by their work. The group was hailed as the Glasgow School of Painting, or, more affectionately, the Glasgow Boys.

Glasgow residents boast they have some of the world's best museums. The Glasgow Art Gallery and Museum holds a superb collection of European masters. The Burrell Collection displays antique furniture and delicate French silverware, all donated by the wealthy shipowner Sir William Burrell. The People's Palace tells the history of Glasgow through paintings and sculptures. In the Museum of Transport stand magnificent automobiles, some almost 100 years old. Expect to hear rich music at the National Museum of Piping, which opened in 1996 and tells the history of the bagpipe.

In 1999, Glasgow was named the United Kingdom's City of Architecture, and it hosted a worldwide gathering of designers and city planners. Its older buildings stand as monuments to a prosperous past. George Square, in the city's center, was laid out in the late 1800s and is anchored by the elegant Merchant City and the City Chambers. A statue of Sir Walter Scott rises on a tall column in George Square. The Glasgow School of Art was designed by one of Scotland's greatest architects, Charles Rennie Mackintosh (1868–1928). Another Mackintosh creation is the Willow Tea Room (completed in 1904), for which the master designed every item

including the restaurant's high-backed chairs. The most revered building in the city is the Glasgow Cathedral, which was first begun in the 1100s.

Glasgow's George Square

Yet a visitor can sense Glasgow's decay in its architecture. Many downtown buildings are abandoned and have boarded-up windows and weeds poking through cracks in the walls. In some neighborhoods stand block after block of drab council flats. Put up mainly in the 1960s, these are the type of faceless high-rise buildings called housing projects in the United States. Most tenants in the council flats are impoverished families. When Glasgow's old factories closed, the unskilled jobs vanished with them. Thousands of Glasgow city dwellers were left behind as Scotland's economy changed from manufacturing to high technology and tourism.

These drab high rise buildings are evidence of Glasgow's urban decay.

Glasgow's Airport is Scotland's biggest. It is also the arrival and departure point for many visitors to the country. Those who leave long to come back. Of course, there is a haunting folk song welcoming people to return to Scotland:

Will you no come back again?
Will you no come back again?
Better loved you'll never be,
Will you no come back again?

An aerial view of Scotland's spectacular landscape

Timeline

Scottish History

James IV marries English princess Margaret Tudor; England and Scotland continue to fight over rule of Scotland.	1503
At Flodden Field, the Scots suffer the worst defeat in their history, in a battle with England.	1513
The Presbyterian Church replaces the Catholic Church as the national church of Scotland.	1560
England's Queen Elizabeth dies, naming Scotland's King James VI as her heir and creating the Personal Union.	1603
Civil war breaks out in England; the Scottish side with the English rebels.	1642
The Act of Union is passed, uniting Scotland, England, and Wales to form Great Britain.	1707
The first Jacobite rebellion breaks out; the Jacobites are defeated.	1715
Prince Charles Edward Stuart, "Bonnie Prince Charlie," leads the second Jacobite rebellion.	1745
Jacobite Scots are slaughtered by Government troops in the Battle of Culloden; Charles escapes to France.	1746
Labor unions force the signing of the Factory Act, restricting child labor.	1838
The Education Act is signed, requiring all children aged five through thirteen to attend school.	1872
The Scottish National Party is formed, calling for separation from the United Kingdom.	1928
The Stone of Destiny, Scotland's coronation stone, is returned from London to Edinburgh Castle, 700 years after being stolen by Edward I.	1996
The Scotland Act is passed in the British Parliament, establishing a separate Scottish Parliament.	1997
A Scottish Parliament is reinstated after 292 years.	1999

World History

1500s	The Reformation leads to the birth of Protestantism.
1776	The Declaration of Independence is signed.
1789	The French Revolution begins.
1865	The American Civil War ends.
1914	World War I breaks out.
1917	The Bolshevik Revolution brings Communism to Russia.
1929	Worldwide economic depression begins.
1939	World War II begins, following the German invasion of Poland.
1957	The Vietnam War starts.
1989	The Berlin Wall is torn down, as Communism crumbles in Eastern Europe.
1996	Bill Clinton is re-elected U.S. president.

Fast Facts

Official name: Scotland

Capital: Edinburgh

Official language: English

Aberdeen

Scotland's flag

A lighthouse sits on the high cliffs of Neist.

Official religion:	Presbyterian (Church of Scotland)
Year of founding:	1314, independence from England
National anthem:	"Flower of Scotland"
Government:	Constitutional monarchy
Chief of state:	British Monarch
Head of government:	Prime minister
Area and dimensions:	30,418 square miles (78,783 sq km) including islands off the coast; 274 miles (441 km) from north to south and varies east to west between 26 miles (42 km) and 154 miles (248 km)
Latitude and longitude of geographic center:	57° 00' N, 4° 00' W
Land and water borders:	North and west: Atlantic Ocean; east: North Sea; south: England
Highest elevation:	Ben Nevis, 4,406 feet (1,343 m)
Lowest elevation:	Sea level, along the coast
Average temperature:	38.6°F (3.7°C) in January and 58.3°F (10.5°C) in July in Edinburgh
Average precipitation:	27 inches (69 cm) in Edinburgh
National population (1995 est.):	5,137,000

Edinburgh Castle

Currency

Population of largest cities (1996 est):		
	Edinburgh	448,850
	Glasgow	616,430
	Aberdeen	217,260
	Dundee	150,250

Famous landmarks:
- ▶ *Edinburgh Castle*
- ▶ *the Royal Mile*
- ▶ *the "Stone of Destiny"*
- ▶ *Holyrood Palace*
- ▶ *Glasgow Cathedral*
- ▶ *Loch Ness*

Industry: Steel, heavy engineering and metal manufacturing, textiles, motor vehicles and aircraft, construction, electronics, chemicals

Currency: Scottish pound sterling, directly tied to British pound sterling. In late 2000, £0.67 = U.S.$1.

System of weights and measures: Metric system

Literacy rate: 100% (1990 est.)

Common Scottish Gaelic words and phrases:

Hallo.	Hello.
Thig a-staigh.	Come in.
Tapadh leat.	Thank you.
An-diugh	Today
An-dé	Yesterday
Mar sin leat.	Goodbye.

Robert Louis Stevenson

Famous Scots:

Sir James Barrie	(1860–1937)	
Author		
Alexander Graham Bell	(1847–1922)	
Inventor		
Robert Burns	(1759–1796)	
Poet		
Sean Connery	(1930–)	
Actor		
Sir Arthur Conan Doyle	(1859–1930)	
Author and creator of the detective Sherlock Holmes		
Sir Alexander Fleming	(1881–1955)	
Scientist		
Kenneth Grahame	(1859–1932)	
Author		
William Kidd (Captain Kidd)	(1645–1701)	
Pirate		
Sir Walter Scott	(1771–1832)	
Writer and poet		
Adam Smith	(1723–1790)	
Economist		
Robert Louis Stevenson	(1850–1894)	
Author		

To Find Out More

Nonfiction

▶ Aman, Catherine. *The Scottish Americans*. People of North America. New York: Chelsea House, 1991.

▶ Arnold, Caroline. *Stone Age Farmers beside the Sea; Scotland's Prehistoric Village of Skara Brae*. New York: Clarion Books, 1997.

▶ Brownstein, Robin. *The Scotch-Irish Americans*. People of North America. New York: Chelsea House, 1988.

▶ Dunlop, Eileen. *Stones of Destiny*. (A Collection of Scottish and Irish Folktales) Chester Springs, Penn.: Dufour Books, 1994.

▶ Humble, Richard. *The Travels of Livingstone*. Exploration through the Ages. Danbury, Conn: Watts, 1991.

▶ Kent, Zachary. *Andrew Carnegie: Steel King and Friend to Libraries*. Berkeley Heights, NJ: Enslow Publishers, 1999.

▶ Martell, Hazel. *The Celts*. New York: Penguin Books, 1994.

▶ Meek, James. *The Land and People of Scotland*. Portrait of the Nations. New York: Harper Childrens Books, 1990.

▶ Taylor, Doreen. *Scotland*. World in View. Chatham, NJ: Raintree Steck-Vaughn, 1990.

Fiction

▶ Duncan, Jane. *Brave Janet Reachfar*. A novel about Scottish farm life. Houghton Books, Boston: 1975.

▶ Dunlop, Eileen. *Finn's Island* A young mainland boy journeys to the Hebrides Islands where his grandfather grew up. Holiday House, New York: 1992.

Poetry

▶ Stevenson, Robert Louis. *A Child's Garden of Verses*. Illustrated Edition. Longmeadow Press, Stamford, Conn., 1994.

Websites

▶ **Scotland.Com**
http://www.scotland.com
A comprehensive look at Scotland.

▶ **The Soc. Culture**
http://www.scot.demon.co.uk/
scotfaq/contents.html
Many elements of Scottish life are covered here, including hints as to how one can trace his or her Scottish ancestors.

▶ **Hidden Scotland**
http://www.hiddenscotland.com
A travel guide to out-of-the-way places in Scotland.

Organizations

▶ **British Embassy**
3100 Massachusetts Avenue
Washington, DC 20008

▶ **Scottish Natural Heritage**
12 Hope Terrace
Edinburgh EH9 2AS
phone: 01-44 131-447 4784
fax: 01-44 131-446 2277

▶ **Scottish Tourist Board**
23 Ravelston Terrace
Edinburgh EH4 3EU
phone: 01-44 131-332 2433
fax: 01-44 131-343 1513

▶ **Historic Scotland**
Longmore House
Salisbury Place
Edinburgh EH9 1SH
phone: 01-44-131-668 8600

Index

Page numbers in *italics* indicate illustrations.

Meet the Author

"Hello. I'm R. Conrad Stein, and I've been writing books for young readers for many, many years. I've published more than 100 books, most of them histories and books about geography. I was born in Chicago. When I was eighteen I joined the Marine Corps and served three years. Later I attended the University of Illinois and graduated with a degree in history. I have worked as a teacher, a merchant seaman, and a truck driver. Since the late 1970s I've been a full-time writer. I now live in Chicago with my wife Deborah Kent (who is also a writer of books for young readers) and our daughter, Janna.

"Traveling is my favorite hobby. I enjoy wandering the streets of strange cities. I don't mind getting lost when I'm in foreign cities because getting lost leads to so many surprises. In the summer of 1999 my wife and I took a thoroughly enjoyable trip to Scotland. We hiked the hills of the Highlands and roamed about castles and historic houses. All the time we talked to the friendly Scottish people. Upon returning I looked forward to writing this book on Scotland."

Photo Credits

Photographs ©:

AllSport USA/Mike Hewitt: 114 bottom;

Britain on View/British Tourist Authority: 120 (Glyn Satterley), 7 top, 15, 91;

Britstock/Cheryl Hogue: 2, 96;

Brown Brothers: 87, 104;

Bryan and Cherry Alexander: 22, 27, 32, 39 top;

Churchill & Klehr Photography: 10, 17 top;

Corbis-Bettmann: 20 (Michael Busselle), 48 top, 68 (Hulton-Deutsch Collection), 28 (Roger Tidman), 100 (Adam Woolfitt), 51, 62, 95, 105 bottom, 133;

Greg Gawlowski: 17 bottom, 21, 73 top, 89, 93 top, 117;

Laurie Campbell: 37 top, 38, 84 top;

Liaison Agency, Inc.: 94 (Remi Benali & Stephen Ferry), 65 (Tom Kidd/FSP), 66 (Stephen Lock/FSP), 79 (Bill Reitzel);

Liaison Agency, Inc./Hulton Getty Archive: 52, 58, 60, 63, 93 bottom;

National Geographic Image Collection/Steve Raymer: 31;

Peter Arnold Inc.: 41 top (John Cancalosi), 116 (Malcolm S. Kirk), 39 bottom (Kevin Schafer), 97 (TomPix);

Photo Researchers, NY: 33 (Angelina Lax), 19, 41 bottom , 114 top (Raphael Macia), 37 bottom (Larry Nicholson), 35 bottom (Hans Reinhard/Okapia);

Photofest: 50;

Scotland in Focus: 86, 132 bottom (G. Davis), 48 bottom, 121 (J. Guidi), 126 (M. Johnston), 76, 118 bottom (G. Satterley), 108 top (R. Schofield), 34 (Phil Seale), 83, 125 (R. Weir), 122 (Willbir), 29, 40;

Sports Illustrated Picture Collection/Simon Bruty: 113 (#5718707);

Stock Montage, Inc.: 46, 54, 69, 101;

Stone: 127 (David Paterson), 14, 131 bottom (Art Wolfe), 9 (Gary Yeowell);

Superstock, Inc.: 55 (Christie's Images), 105 top (National Portrait Gallery, London), 26 (Stock Montage), 13, 45;

The Image Works: 7 bottom, 42, 118 top (Bachmann), 106 (William Conran), 44 bottom (M. Everton), 102 (John Griffin), 73 bottom, 108 bottom (Snider);

The Image Works/Topham Picturepoint: 115 (Michael Serraillier), 24, 49, 81, 130 left;

Tiofoto: 71, 132 top (Jan Rietz), cover, 3 (Mats Rosenberg);

Viesti Collection, Inc.: 110 (Walter Bibikow), 25 (Eric A. Wessman);

Visuals Unlimited: 112 (Cheryl Hogue), 35 top (Joe McDonald);

Woodfin Camp & Associates: 78 (Nathan Benn), 88, 98 (Catherine Karnow), 8, 30, 44 top (Adam Woolfitt).

Maps by Joe LeMonnier.